Temporal Data Mining via Unsupervised Ensemble Learning

Temporal Data Mining via Unsupervised Ensemble Learning

Yun Yang

ELSEVIER

AMSTERDAM • BOSTON • HEIDELBERG • LONDON
NEW YORK • OXFORD • PARIS • SAN DIEGO
SAN FRANCISCO • SINGAPORE • SYDNEY • TOKYO

Elsevier

Radarweg 29, PO Box 211, 1000 AE Amsterdam, Netherlands

The Boulevard, Langford Lane, Kidlington, Oxford OX5 1GB, United Kingdom

50 Hampshire Street, 5th Floor, Cambridge, MA 02139, United States

Library of Congress Cataloging-in-Publication Data
A catalog record for this book is available from the Library of Congress

British Library Cataloguing-in-Publication Data
A catalogue record for this book is available from the British Library

ISBN: 978-0-12-811654-8

For information on all Elsevier publications visit our website at https://www.elsevier.com/

Working together to grow libraries in developing countries

www.elsevier.com • www.bookaid.org

Publisher: Glyn Jones
Acquisition Editor: Glyn Jones
Editorial Project Manager: Naomi Robertson
Production Project Manager: Kiruthika Govindaraju
Cover Designer: Miles Hitchen

Typeset by TNQ Books and Journals

Contents

List of Figures

List of Tables

Acknowledgments

First of all, the author would like to thank his parents for their boundless love and encouragement, not to mention their grit and tenacity they have shown him for dealing with any problem, their fortitude through tough time strongly inspires his life and has instilled in him the inner strength and determination which is vital to the completion of this book.

Also the author is grateful to Eamonn Keogh who provided the Benchmark time series data set for evaluating their proposed models; Alexander Strehl who published his Cluster Ensemble code online in helping him to complete the comparative studies shown in this book.

Finally, the author wishes to acknowledge the financial support from the Chinese Natural Science Foundation (CNSF) under the grant number: 61402397 and grant number: 61663046, Yunnan Applied Fundamental Research Project under the grant number: 2016FB104, Yunnan Key Laboratory of Software Engineering General Program under the grant number: 2015SE201, and Yunnan High Level Overseas Talent Recruitment Program.

Introduction

1

CHAPTER OUTLINE

1.1 BACKGROUND

The unsupervised classification or clustering provides an effective way to condensing and summarizing information conveyed in data, which is demanded by a number of application areas for organizing or discovering structures in data. The objective of clustering analysis is to partition a set of unlabeled objects into groups or clusters where all the objects grouped in the same cluster should be coherent or homogeneous. There are two core problems in clustering analysis; that is, model selection and proper grouping. The former is seeking a solution that estimates the intrinsic number of clusters underlying a data set, while the latter demands a rule to group coherent objects together to form a cluster. From the perspective of machine learning, clustering analysis is an extremely difficult unsupervised learning task since it is inherently an ill-posed problem and its solution often violates some common assumptions (Kleinberg, 2003). There have been many researches in clustering analysis (Jain et al., 1999), which leads to various clustering algorithms categorized as partitioning, hierarchical, density-based, and model-based clustering algorithms.

Actually, temporal data are a collection of observations associated with information such as the time at which data have been captured and the time interval during which a data value is valid. Temporal data are composed of a sequence of nominal symbols from the alphabet known as a temporal sequence and a sequence of continuous real-valued elements known as a time series. The use of temporal data have become widespread in recent years, and temporal data mining continues to be a rapidly evolving area of interrelated disciplines including statistics, temporal pattern recognition, temporal databases, optimization, visualization, high-performance computing, and parallel computing.

Temporal Data Mining via Unsupervised Ensemble Learning. http://dx.doi.org/10.1016/B978-0-12-811654-8.00001-4

However, the recent empirical studies in temporal data analysis reveal that most of the existing clustering algorithms do not work well for temporal data due to their special structure and data dependency (Keogh and Kasetty, 2003), which presents a big challenge in clustering temporal data of various and high dimensionality, large volume, very high-feature correlation, and a substantial amount of noise.

Recently, several studies have attempted to improve clustering by combining multiple clustering solutions into a single-consolidated clustering ensemble for better average performance among given clustering solutions. This has led to many real-world applications, including gene classification, image segmentation (Hong et al., 2008), video retrieval, and so on (Jain et al., 1999; Fischer and Buhmann, 2003; Azimi et al., 2006). Clustering ensembles usually involve two stages. First, multiple partitions are obtained through several runs of initial clustering analysis. Subsequently, the specific consensus function is used in order to find a final consensus partition from multiple input partitions. This book is going to concentrate on ensemble learning techniques and its application for temporal data clustering tasks based on three methodologies: the model-based approach, the proximity-based approach, and the feature-based approach.

The model-based approach aims to construct statistical models to describe the characteristics of each group of temporal data, providing more intuitive ways to capture dynamic behaviors and a more flexible means for dealing with the variable lengths of temporal data. In general, the entire temporal data set is modeled by a mixture of these statistical models, while an individual statistical model such as Gaussian distribution, Poisson distribution, or Hidden Markov Model (HMM) is used to model a specific cluster of temporal data. Model-based approaches for temporal data clustering include HMM (Panuccio et al., 2009), Gaussian mixture model (Fraley and Raftery, 2002), mixture of first-order Markov chain (Smyth, 1999), dynamic Bayesian networks (Murphy, 2002), and autoregressive moving average model (Xiong and Yeung, 2002). Usually, these are combined with an expectation-maximization algorithm (Bilmes, 1998) for parameter estimation.

The proximity-based approach is mainly based on the measure of the similarity or distance between each pair of temporal data. The most common methods are agglomerative and divisive clustering (Jain et al., 1999), which partition the unlabeled objects into different groups so that members of the same groups are more alike than members of different groups based on the similarity metric. For proximity-based clustering, either the Euclidean distance or an advanced version of Mahalanobis distance (Bar-Hillel et al., 2006) would be commonly used as the basis for comparing the similarity of two sets of temporal data.

The feature-based approach is indirect temporal data clustering, which begins with the extraction of a set of features from raw temporal data, so that all temporal data can be transformed into a static feature space. Then, classical vector-based clustering algorithms can be implemented within the feature space. Obviously, feature extraction is the essential factor that decides the performance of clustering. Generally, feature-based clustering reduces the computational complexities for higher dimensional temporal data.

1.2 **PROBLEM STATEMENT**

Although the clustering algorithms have been intensively developing for last decades, due to the natural complexity of temporal data, we still face many challenges for temporal data clustering tasks.

How to select an intrinsic number of clusters is still a critical model selection problem existing in many clustering algorithms. In a statistical framework, model selection is the task of selecting a mixture of the appropriate number of mathematical models with the appropriate parameter setup that fits the target data set by optimizing some criterion. In other words, the model selection problem is solved by optimizing the predefined criterion. For common model selection criterion, Akaike information criterion, AIC (Akaike, 1974), balances the good fit of a statistical model based on maximum log-likelihood and model complexity based on the number of model parameters. The optimal number of clusters is selected with a minimum value of AIC. Based on Bayesian model selection principles, the Bayesian information criterion, BIC (Schwarz, 1978), is a similar approach to AIC. However, while the number of parameters and maximum log-likelihood are required to compute the AIC, the computation of BIC requires the number of observations and maximum log-likelihood instead. Monte-Carlo cross validation (Smyth, 1996) divides a data set into training and test sets at certain times in a random manner. In each run, the training set is used to estimate the best-fitting parameters while the testing set computes the model's error. The optimal number of clusters is selected by posteriori probabilities or criterion function. Recently, the Bayesian Ying-Yang machine (Xu, 1996) has been applied to model selection in clustering analysis (Xu, 1997). It treats the unsupervised learning problem as a problem of estimating the joint distribution between the observable pattern in the observable space and its representation pattern in the representation space. In theory, the optimal number of clusters is given by the minimum value of cost function. In addition, other criterions of model selection include minimum message length (Grunwald et al., 1998), minimum description length (Grunwald et al., 1998), and covariance inflation criterion (Tibshirani and Knight, 1999). However, recent empirical studies (Zucchini, 2000; Hu and Xu, 2003) in model selection reveal that most of the existing criterions have different limitations, which often overestimate or underestimate the cluster number. Performance of these different criterions depends on the structure of the target data set, and no single criterion emerges as outstanding when measured against the others. Moreover, a major problem associated with these model selection criterions also remains: the computation procedures involved are extremely complex and time consuming.

How to significantly reduce the computational cost is another importance issue for temporal data clustering task due to the fact of that temporal data are often collected in a data set with large volume, high and various dimensionality, and complex-clustered structure. From the perspective of model-based temporal data clustering, Zhong and Ghosh (2003) proposed a model-based hybrid partitioning-hierarchical clustering and its variance such as HHM-based hierarchical meta clustering. In the first approach, one is an improved version of model-based agglomerative clustering, which keeps some hierarchical structure. However, associating with HMM-based K-models clustering, the complexity of input data to the agglomerative clustering is relatively reduces. Therefore, this approach requires less computational cost. Moreover, the HHM-based hierarchical meta clustering further reduces the computational cost due to no re-estimation of merged component models as a composite model. However, both of them are still quite time consuming in comparison to most proximity-based and representation-based approaches. Furthermore, the aforementioned model selection problem is still unavoidable. From the perspective of proximity-based temporal data clustering, K-means algorithm is effective in clustering large-scale data sets, and efforts have been made in order to overcome its disadvantages (Huang, 1998; Ordonez and Omiecinski, 2004), which potentially provides a clustering solution for temporal with large volume. Sampling-based approach such as Clustering LARge Applications (CLARA) (Kaufman and Rousseeuw, 1990) and Clustering Using REpristentatives (CURE) (Guha et al., 1998) reduces the computational cost by applying an appropriate sampling technique on the entire data set with large volume. Condensation-based approach such as Balanced Iterative Reducing and Clustering using Hierarchies (BIRCH) (Zhang et al., 1996) constructs the compact summaries of the original data in a Cluster Feature (CF) tree, which captures the clustering information and significantly reduces the computational burden. Density-based approach such as Densit-based Spatial Clustering of Application with Noise (DBSCAN) (Ester et al., 1996) Ordering Points To Identify the Clustering Structure (OPTICS) (Ankerst et al., 1999) is able to automatically determine the complex clustered structure by finding the dense area of data set. Although each algorithm has a good performance for clustering large volume of data set, most of them have the difficulty to deal with temporal data with various length. From the perspective of representation-based temporal data clustering, the computational cost can be significantly reduced by projecting the temporal data with various length and high dimensionality into a uniform lower dimensional representation space, where most of the existing clustering algorithms can be applied. However, our previous study (Yang and Chen, 2011a) has shown that no single representation technique could perfectly represent all the different temporal data set, each of them just capture limited amount of characters obtained from temporal data set.

How to thoroughly extract the important features from original temporal data is concerned with the representation methods. Nowadays, various representations have been proposed for temporal data (Faloutsos et al., 1994 Dimitrova and Golshani, 1995; Chen and Chang, 2000; Keogh et al., 2001; Chakrabarti et al., 2002; Bashir, 2005; Cheong et al., 2005; Bagnall et al., 2006; Gionis et al., 2007; Ding et al., 2008; Ye and Keogh, 2009), and its variants such as the multiple-scaled representation (Lin et al., 2004) continues to be proposed for improving the temporal data clustering performance. Nevertheless, one representation tends to encode only those features well presented in its representation space, which inevitably causes the loss of other useful information conveyed in the original temporal data. Due to the high complexity and varieties of temporal data, to our knowledge, there is no universal representation that perfectly characterizes miscellaneous temporal data. Therefore, a representation is merely applicable to a class of temporal data where their salient features can be fully captured in the representation space but such information is hardly available without prior knowledge and a careful analysis. Therefore, the alternative approaches have been developed for use of different representations. They are simply lumping different representations together to constitute a composite representation (Li and Wrench, 1983; Attili et al., 1988; Openshaw et al., 1993; Colombi et al., 1996) and directly apply clustering analysis on the composite representation. Although such an approach could reduce the computational cost, it leads to a higher dimensional feature vector of redundancy, and different representations get involved in different measure criteria, and so it is a nontrivial issue on how to normalize different representations to form a composite representation.

1.3 OBJECTIVE OF BOOK

A large of number of recent studies have shown that unsupervised ensemble approaches improve clustering quality by combining multiple clustering solutions into a single consolidated clustering ensemble that has the best performance among given clustering solutions. As a result, ensemble learning techniques may give an optimal solution of dealing with temporal data clustering problems. During the last 10 years, the author was trying to solve the problems of temporal data clustering via ensemble learning approaches and produced some excellent research works including proposing and developing several innovation methods and algorithms. However, as he works on the subject, he has been aware that there is just a little literature of presenting unsupervised ensemble learning with a focus on its application to temporal data clustering. Therefore, he published this book to fill the need for a comprehensive guide on the subject. This book will not only give an overview of temporal data mining, in-depth knowledge of temporal data clustering, and ensemble learning techniques in an accessible format designed to appeal to students and professional researchers with little mathematical and statistical background but also have a rich blend of theory and practice with three proposed novel approaches:

- HMM, an important model-based approach for temporal data clustering, has been studied. The author proposes a novel approach based on the ensemble of HMM-based partitioning clustering associated with hierarchical clustering refinement in order to solve problems in finding the intrinsic number of clusters and model initialization problems which exist in most model-based clustering algorithms.
- Proximity-based approaches pose real challenges of computational cost in temporal data clustering due to the large volume of temporal data. In this book, author presents an unsupervised ensemble learning model of iteratively

constructed partitions on the subtraining set obtained by a hybrid sampling scheme. The proposed approach not only reduces the computational cost of temporal data clustering but also obtains a more general framework for any type of data clustering analysis, which provides a potential solution for large temporal data clustering tasks.

- Feature-based approach to temporal data clustering is proposed through a weighted ensemble of a simple clustering algorithm with minimum user-dependent parameters, such as k-means with different representations, in order to address both proper grouping with minimum computational cost and selecting an intrinsic number of clusters as model selection problems in clustering analysis as a whole. This proposed approach takes into account the diversity of partitions generated by certain clustering algorithm on different representations, initial and reconciles them in an optimal way. Furthermore, the proposed weighted consensus function not only enables automatic model selection for clustering analysis but also provides a generic technique for the optimal solution of combining multiple partitions.

Furthermore, readers will realize that each of temporal clustering approaches favor differently structured temporal data or types of temporal data with certain assumptions. There is nothing universal that can solve all problems, and it is important to understand the characteristics of both clustering algorithms and the target temporal data.

1.4 OVERVIEW OF BOOK

This book is enlightening for students and researchers wishing to study on temporal data mining and unsupervised ensemble learning approaches. It is not only to enumerate the existing techniques proposed so far but also to classify and organize them in a way that may be of help for a practitioner looking for solutions to a concrete problem. Furthermore, author also provides some of novel unsupervised ensemble learning approaches for temporal data clustering in this book. This book is organized as follows:

In Chapter 2, a review of temporal data mining is carried out from three aspects. Initially, representation of temporal data are reviewed, followed by similarity measures of temporal data mining based on different objectives, and then five mining tasks including prediction, classification, clustering, search and retrieval, and pattern discovery are briefly described at the end of chapter.

In Chapter 3, we present a comprehensive survey on temporal data clustering algorithms from different perspectives, which includes partitional clustering, hierarchical clustering, density-based clustering, and model-based clustering. Their strengths and weakness are also discussed for temporal data clustering tasks. Moreover, based on the internal, external, and relative criteria, most common clustering validity indices are described for quantitative evaluation of clustering quality.

In Chapter 4, a systemic literature of ensemble leaning is presented in two parts. First, we discuss the ensemble learning from three aspects: ensemble learning algorithms, combining methods, and diversity of ensemble learning. By giving in-depth knowledge about unsupervised ensemble learning, we further discuss the consensus functions and objective functions of clustering ensemble approaches.

In Chapter 5, HMM model-based framework is detailed with related works. We discuss the problems of existing HMM model-based clustering algorithms and present a novel HMM-based ensemble clustering approach. Such approach is designed to solve the problems in finding the intrinsic number of clusters and model initialization sensitivity. This approach has been compared with several similar approaches and evaluated on synthetic data, time series benchmark, and motion trajectory database and yields promising results for clustering tasks.

In Chapter 6, we initially have a brief analysis on sampling-based ensemble approaches including both boosting and bagging and identify the major differences between both of ensemble learning approaches. Then, inspired by both boosting and bagging, an iteratively constructed clustering ensemble model is proposed by combining the strengths of both boosting and bagging. The proposed approach is also evaluated on synthetic data, time series benchmark, and real-world motion trajectory data sets, and experimental results show satisfactory performance for a variety of clustering tasks.

In Chapter 7, we present a weighted clustering ensemble of multiple partitions produced by initial clustering analysis on different temporal data representations. This approach is designed to solve the problems in finding the intrinsic number of clusters, sensitivity to initialization, and combination method of ensemble learning. It also provides a tradeoff solution between computational cost and accuracy for temporal data clustering. To demonstrate effectiveness, the proposed approach is applied to a variety of temporal data clustering tasks, including benchmark time series, motion trajectory, and time-series data stream clustering. The experimental results and their analyses are stated. A detailed discussion of future works concludes this chapter.

In Chapter 8, the work presented in the book is summarized. The three proposed ensemble models are reviewed and analyzed, and then final conclusions are drawn. Unsolved problems are also discussed with regard to their potential for future research work.

Temporal Data Mining

2

CHAPTER OUTLINE

2.1 INTRODUCTION

Temporal data mining can be defined as "process of knowledge discovery in temporal databases that enumerates structures (temporal patterns or models) over the temporal data, and any algorithm that enumerates temporal patterns from, or fits models to, temporal data is a temporal data mining algorithm" (Lin et al., 2002). The aim of temporal data mining is to discover temporal patterns, unexpected trends, or other hidden relations in the larger sequential data, which is composed of a sequence of nominal symbols from the alphabet known as a temporal sequence and a sequence of continuous real-valued elements known as a time series, by using a combination of techniques from machine learning, statistics, and database technologies. In fact, temporal data mining is composed of three major works including representation of temporal data, definition of similarity measures and mining tasks.

Temporal Data Mining via Unsupervised Ensemble Learning. http://dx.doi.org/10.1016/B978-0-12-811654-8.00002-6

9

2.2 REPRESENTATIONS OF TEMPORAL DATA

Representation of temporal data refers to how to represent the temporal data in an efficient way before actually mining operations takes place. There are three major methods: time domain—based representations, transformation-based representations, and generative model—based representations.

2.2.1 TIME DOMAIN—BASED REPRESENTATIONS

Time domain—based representations are the simplest way to represent the temporal data with minimal manipulation. It can keep either the original form of temporal data that is a sequence of initial samples ordered in their occurrence within the time domain or segment the temporal sequence into several parts, where each of segmentations is represented by linear functions. Generally, the time domain—based representations has the advantages of easy implementation and preventing from losing information obtained from temporal data. However, it potentially requires demanding computational power and memory resource for the mining operations and may become infeasible for the real-world applications involving the temporal data with large volume and high dimensionality.

2.2.2 TRANSFORMATION-BASED REPRESENTATIONS

Transformation-based representations aim to transfer the original temporal data into a representation space, where those features that contain the most discriminatory information are extracted and used for representing the temporal data. In general, such representations can be classified into two categories: piecewise and global representations. A piecewise representation is generated by partitioning the temporal data into segments at critical points based on a criterion then each segment will be modeled into a concise representation. As a result, all segment representations constitute a piecewise representation collectively, for example, adaptive piecewise constant approximation (Chakrabarti et al., 2002) and curvature-based Principal Component Analysis (PCA) segments (Bashir, 2005). On the other hand, a global representation is derived by modeling the temporal data via a set of basic functions, and therefore, coefficients in the parameter space forms a global representation that can be used to reconstruct the temporal data approximately. The commonly used global representations are polynomial/spline curve fitting (Dimitrova and Golshani, 1995; Chen and Chang, 2000), discrete Fourier transforms (DFTs) (Faloutsos et al., 1994), discrete wavelet transforms (DWTs) (Sahouria and Zakhor, 1997). The major advantage of transformation-based representations is to reduce high, even various dimensional temporal data to uniform lower dimensional feature space, which significantly improves computational efficiency. However, based on our previous study (Yang, 2006; Yang and Chen, 2006, 2007), we realized that no single representation technique could perfectly represent all the different temporal data set, each of them just capture limited amount of characters obtained from temporal data set.

There follow reviews of the two piecewise and two global representations applied in our proposed algorithm—Weighted clustering ensemble with multiple representations presented in Chapter 7: piecewise local statistics (PLS), piecewise discrete wavelet transform (PDWT), polynomial curve fitting (PCF), and DFTs.

Piecewise Local Statistics

Motivated by the short-term analysis in speech signal processing, discovery of time series motifs (Lin et al., 2002), and a bit-level representation of time series (Bagnall et al., 2006), we adopt a window-based statistical analysis for time series. First of all, we use a window of the fixed size to block time series into a set of segments. For each segment, we estimate the first- and second-order statistics used features of this segment. For segment n, its local statistics, mean μ_n, and standard deviation σ_n of observations are estimated by

$$\mu_n = \frac{1}{|W|} \sum_{t=1+(n-1)|W|}^{n|W|} x(t), \quad \sigma_n = \sqrt{\frac{1}{|W|} \sum_{t=1+(n-1)|W|}^{n|W|} [x(t) - \mu_n]^2} \quad (2.1)$$

where $|W|$ is the size of the window. For time series, a PLS representation of a fixed dimension is formed by the collective notation of local statistic features of all segments though the estimate might be affected at the end of time series where the window is delimited. The PLS representation would be an extension of the representation proposed in Keogh et al. (2001) where the first-order statistics only is used.

Piecewise Discrete Wavelet Transforms

DWT turns out to be an effective multiscale analysis tool. Like the preprocessing in the PLS representation, time series, $\{x(t)\}_{t=1}^{T}$, is blocked into a set of segments with a window of size $|W|$. In the proposed weighted clustering ensemble model presented in Chapter 7, we apply the Daubechies wavelets to each segment for a multiscale analysis in order to capture local details in a more accurate way, for example, abrupt changes, that often fail to be characterized accurately by local statistics in our PLS representation. For the nth segment with a multiscale analysis of J levels, the application of the DWT leads to a piecewise representation with all coefficients collectively:

$$\{x(t)\}_{t=(n-1)|W|}^{n|W|} \Rightarrow \left\{ \Psi_L^J, \left\{ \Psi_H^j \right\}_{j=1}^{J} \right\} \quad (2.2)$$

The DWT decomposes each segment of time series via the successive use of low-pass and high-pass filtering at appropriate levels. At level j, $|W| * 2^{-j}$ coefficients of high-pass filters, Ψ_H^j, encode the detailed information, while those of low-pass filters, Ψ_L^j, characterize coarse information.

Polynomial Curve Fitting

The objective of curve fitting is to find a mathematical equation that describes the signal and that is minimally influenced by the presence of noise. The most common approach is the least-squares polynomial method, which is capable of finding the coefficients of polynomial equations that are a best fit to the sequential data. In the study by Policker and Geva (2000), time series is modeled by fitting it to a parametric polynomial function

$$x(t) = \alpha_P t^P + \alpha_{P-1} t^{P-1} + \cdots + \alpha_1 t + \alpha_0. \tag{2.3}$$

Here α_p ($p = 0, 1, \ldots, P$) is the polynomial coefficient of the pth order. In general, fourth order of polynomial coefficient gives best performance according the empirical study, higher order does not make significant improvements. The fitting is carried out by minimizing a least-square error function by considering all sequential points of time series and the polynomial model of a given order, with respect to α_p ($p = 0, 1, \ldots, P$). All coefficients obtained via optimization constitute a PCF representation, a sequential point location-dependent global representation of time series. Normally, the complex structure of time series, which has a large amount of abrupt changes along the observed points, would require the higher order polynomial curve for appropriate approximation. Although the PCF is only good at obtaining the global information from time series, the important local information such as the abrupt changes could not be captured by the PCF.

Discrete Fourier Transforms

The previous PCF representation bears the general information of time series trend, which analyze the trajectory in time domain. However, Fourier transform decomposes the time series in frequency domain. The Fourier analysis is among the most widely used tools for transforming data sequences and functions, from the time domain to their representation in the frequency domain. Analysis of sequences in the frequency domain, can uncover important properties which are not readily observable in the time domain. Basically, the Fourier transforms are classified into continues Fourier transform and DFT. The continuous Fourier transform decomposes a continuous waveform into a continuous spectrum of its frequency components, and the inverse transform synthesizes a function from its spectrum of frequency components. In contrast, the DFT is defined for discrete sampled single. For the purpose of temporal data representation, based on discrete sequences of observations from time series, we are particularly interested in the DFT. The DFT maps a discrete sequence in the time domain (observations) to a discrete sequence in the frequency domain (frequency coefficients).

DFTs have been applied to derive a global representation of time series in frequency domain (Faloutsos et al., 1994). The DFT of time series $\{x(t)\}_{t=1}^{T}$ yields a set of Fourier coefficients:

$$a_k = \frac{1}{T} \sum_{t=1}^{T} x(t) \exp\left(\frac{-j2\pi kt}{T}\right), \quad k = 0, 1, \ldots, T - 1 \tag{2.4}$$

In order to form a robust representation in the presence of noise, only few top K ($K \ll T$) coefficients corresponding to low frequencies are collectively used to form a Fourier descriptor, a sequential point location independent global representation of time series. According to our previous study, top 16 coefficients corresponding to low frequencies generally capture most of feature obtained from frequency component; more DFT coefficients do not make significant improvements.

2.2.3 GENERATIVE MODEL–BASED REPRESENTATIONS

Generative model–based representations treat that the temporal data are obtained from a statistical or deterministic model such as Hidden Markov Model (HMM), mixture of first-order Markov chain (Smyth, 1999), dynamic Bayesian networks (Murphy, 2002), or Autoregressive Moving Average Model—ARMA (Xiong and Yeung, 2002), hence entire temporal data set can be represented by a mixture of these models with appropriate model parameters, which is as,

$$p(x|\theta) = \sum_{k=1}^{K} w_k p(x|\theta_k) \tag{2.5}$$

where $\theta = \{\theta_k\}_{k=1}^{K}$ is the unknown model parameters, w_k is the prior probability (also known as mixing or weighting coefficient), and satisfies the requirements $0 \leq w_k \leq 1$, and $\sum_{k=1}^{K} w_k = 1$. K is the number of component models used for representing the entire data set.

As an important model-based representation approach, HMM has outstanding ability in capturing temporal features whose values change significantly during the observation period, thereby satisfying the Markov property. Essentially, temporal data can be represented by the HMM model, which describes an unobservable stochastic process consisting of a finite number of states, each of which is related to another stochastic process that emits observation. Initially, an observation is emitted with an emission probability b_j at the state j, which is selected according to the initial probability π_j. The next state i is decided by the state transition probability a_{ij} and also generates a symbol based on emission probability b_i. The process repeats until reaching a stop criterion. The entire process produces a sequence of observations instead of states, from where the name "hidden" is drawn. The complete set of model parameters describing HMM are given by the triplet $\lambda = \{\pi, A, B\}$, where $\pi = \{\pi_j\}$, $A = \{a_{ij}\}$, $B = \{b_j\}$. For continuous-valued temporal data such as time series, the emission probability function of each state is defined by multivariate Gaussian distribution. However, for application of HMM involved in our simulations, the emission distribution function of continuous-valued temporal data is normally modeled as a single Gaussian distribution $b_j = \{\mu_j, \sigma_j^2\}$ in order to reduce the computational cost and prevent the risk of overfitting on the limited available data set.

For temporal data, the entire data set can be represented as a set of K HMM $\{\lambda_1, \lambda_2, ..., \lambda_K\}$ with M states based on single Gaussian distributed observations. Each component consists of the following parameters:

- An M-dimensional initial state probability vector π
- An $M \times M$ state transition matrix A
- Mean vector $\{\mu_1, \mu_2, ..., \mu_M\}$
- Variance vector $\left\{\sigma_1^2, \sigma_2^2, ..., \sigma_M^2\right\}$

For most applications of HMM, we have to solve three major problems:

1. Given the model parameters $\lambda = \{\pi, A, B\}$, compute the probability $p(x|\lambda)$ of a particular sequence of observations $x = \{x(t)\}_{t=1}^T$. This problem is solved by the forward and backward algorithms (Baum and Eagon, 1967; Baum and Sell, 1968).
2. Given the model parameters $\lambda = \{\pi, A, B\}$, find the most likely sequence of hidden states which could have generated a given sequence of observations $x = \{x(t)\}_{t=1}^T$. Solved by the Viterbi algorithm (Viterbi, 1967; Forney Jr., 1973).
3. Given a sequence of observations $x = \{x(t)\}_{t=1}^T$, find the most likely model parameters $\lambda = \{\pi, A, B\}$. Solved by the expectation-maximization algorithm (Dempster et al., 1977).

It is obvious that the HMM-based representation of temporal data could be achieved by solving problem 3.

Although the nature of generative model−based representations would facilitate to identify the data dependency and regularity behind the dynamic behaviors of temporal data, this approach always causes the high-computational cost resulted in mining operations for temporal data with high dimensionality and large volume. Therefore, it may become infeasible in the real-world applications.

2.3 SIMILARITY MEASURES

Once an appropriate representation obtained from temporal data, another interesting problem is to find whether the different temporal data behaves similarly in the representation space, which is referred to similarity measure. Although many similarity measures have been proposed for temporal data mining, there is a strong relation between the representation method and definition of similarity measure, which is mainly governed by the objectives of mining operations. As suggested by Bagnall and Janacek (2005), the similarity measures can be classified into three categories based on different objectives, which are Similarity in time, Similarity in shape and Similarity in change.

2.3.1 SIMILARITY IN TIME

Normally the aim of similarity measures is primarily to measure the similarity between two temporal data related to time and find whether the value of instance varies similarly on each of time intervals. This objective can be achieved by applying a correlation or Euclidean distance metric on the either time domain−based representations or transformation-based representations of temporal data.

Euclidean distance metric has been used for the similarity measure involved in our proposed algorithms that are Iteratively constructed clustering ensemble presented in Chapter 5 and Weighted clustering ensemble with multiple representations presented in Chapter 7. For Iteratively constructed clustering ensemble, we treat the sequence of instance value obtained from original temporal data with identical length as a vector and directly calculate the Euclidean distance between pair of temporal data. For Weighted clustering ensemble with multiple representations, a feature vector is extracted from original temporal data by the corresponding transformation-based representation method; therefore, we simply calculate the Euclidean distance between their feature vector representing the temporal data instead of the original form of temporal data. The Euclidean distance metric is defined as following:

$$D(x, y) = \sqrt{(x, y) \Sigma^{-1} (x - y)^T}, \tag{2.6}$$

where $x = \{x(t)\}_{t=1}^T$ and $y = \{y(t)\}_{t=1}^T$ represent a pair of temporal data with length of T.

2.3.2 SIMILARITY IN SHAPE

Actually similarity in sharp is a more general case of similarity in time, its objective is more likely to find the similarity between two temporal data varied in time or speed by detecting common trend occurred at different time or similar subpattern in the data, for example, finding the similar motion path from several persons who are walking at different speed or time duration. As well known, Dynamic time warping is always used in order to achieve this objective of similarity measure on the temporal data.

In general, Dynamic time warping aims to align pair of sequences such as time series following a warping path so that predetermined distance metric such as Euclidean distance is minimized. Given two time series $x = \{x(i)\}_{i=1}^I$ and $y = \{y(j)\}_{j=1}^J$, the warping path, $z = \{z_l\}_{l=1}^L$ $(\max(I, J) \leq L \leq I + J - 1)$ can be constructed by satisfy three conditions:

1. **Boundary condition:** $z_1 = \{x(1), y(1)\}$ and $z_L = \{x(I), y(J)\}$, this requires the warping path to start and finish at beginning and end instances between two sequences.
2. **Continuity condition:** given $z_l = \{x(i), y(j)\}$ then $z_{l-1} = \{x(i'), y(j')\}$ where $i - i' \leq 1$ and $j - j' \leq 1$. This restricts the allowable steps in the warping path to adjacent manner.
3. **Monotonicity condition:** given $z_l = \{x(i), y(j)\}$ then $z_{l-1} = \{x(i'), y(j')\}$ where $i - i \geq 0$ and $j - j' \geq 0$. This forces the pair of instances in Z to be monotonically spaced in time.

Then the DTW distance can be defined as following:

$$D^{DWT}(x,y) = \min\left(\frac{1}{L}\sum_{l=1}^{L} D^{Euclidean}(z_l)\right) \qquad (2.7)$$

2.3.3 SIMILARITY IN CHANGE

The objective of similar in change is to find the similar dynamic behavior between temporal data whose values change significantly during the observation period. As mentioned in Section 2.2.3, some of generative model−based representations such as HMM and ARMA have outstanding ability in capturing such character. Based on the log-likelihood of each sequence given the model generated for the other sequence, a symmetric distance between two sequences $x = \{x(t)\}_{t=1}^{T}$ and $y = \{y(t)\}_{t=1}^{T}$ has been proposed by Juang and Rabiner (1985), its equation is shown as following:

$$D^{sym}(x,y) = \frac{1}{2}\left[LL_{xy} + LL_{yx}\right] \qquad (2.8)$$

Alternatively, Panuccio et al. (2009) introduced a similar log-likelihood-based distance metric named BP, which is formulated by:

$$D^{BP}(x,y) = \frac{1}{2}\left[\frac{LL_{xy} - LL_{xx}}{LL_{xx}} - \frac{LL_{xy} + LL_{yy}}{LL_{yy}}\right] \qquad (2.9)$$

where $LL_{xy} = \log(p(X|\theta_y))$, given the parameters θ_y of model generating sequence $y = \{y(t)\}_{t=1}^{T}$.

Based on the log-likelihood of each sequence given the corresponding generator model and another model, the Kullback-Leibler (KL) distance (Juang and Rabiner, 1985; Sinkkonen and Kaski, 2002) between both of component models can be computed by using the single linkage, complete linkage, and average linkage methods (Zhong and Ghosh, 2003), which are defined as

$$D^{MinKL}(\lambda_i, \lambda_j) = \min_{x \in C_i}(\log p(x|\lambda_i) - \log p(x|\lambda_j)) \qquad (2.10)$$

$$D^{MaxKL}(\lambda_i, \lambda_j) = \max_{x \in C_i}(\log p(x|\lambda_i) - \log p(x|\lambda_j)) \qquad (2.11)$$

$$D^{BoundaryKL}(\lambda_i, \lambda_j) = \frac{1}{|B_x|}\sum_{x \in C_i}(\log p(x|\lambda_i) - \log p(x|\lambda_j)) \qquad (2.12)$$

where x is the item grouped into the cluster C_i. B_x is the fraction of items x grouped into the cluster C_i that has smallest value $\log p(x|\lambda_x) - \log p(x|\lambda_y)$ and the value of 0 for $\log p(x|\lambda_i) - \log p(x|\lambda_j)$ determines the boundary between cluster i and j.

2.4 **MINING TASKS**

After representing the temporal data in a suitable form and defining the appropriate similarity measure, An algorithm would be used for a particular temporal data task, which is also called mining operation. According to various objectives of temporal data tasks based on a wide range of applications, Lin et al. (2002) suggest that these tasks can be classified into five categories: prediction, classification, clustering, search & retrieval, and pattern discovery. However, the work presented in this book mainly focuses on clustering task.

Prediction: It is one of the most important problems in mining operations, which has to do with forecasting the evolution of temporal data such as time series based on its past samples. In order to do this, generative models are normally built for representing the predictive temporal data. However, in many cases, prediction problems may be formulated as classification, association rule finding, or clustering problems.

Classification: It is one of the most typical operations in supervised learning, but most of classification algorithms have been adapted with special treatment due to the nature of temporal data. In temporal data classification, each data presented to the system are assumed to belong to one of finitely many classes or categories, which are predefined or trained on the given training sets, and these tasks aim to automatically determine the corresponding class or category for the given input data.

Clustering: It is to partition a collection of time series into several groups called clusters such that items with similar characteristics are grouped together. Because clustering provides an unsupervized leaning approach to automatically determine the underlying structure in temporal data that would be always difficult to summarize or visualize due to the nature of temporal data such as large volume, high dimensionality, it has been specially paid attention by many researchers and applied for a wide range of applications. There are two major problems in clustering: finding the intrinsic clusters numbers and properly grouping the temporal data based on a meaningful similarity measure.

Search and retrieval: It can be simply defined as detecting an objective activity from large archives in a general term, but searching for temporal data in large databases is becoming an important task in temporal data mining due to the dramatic growth of temporal data in our daily life. Temporal data search and retrieval techniques play an important role in interactive explorations of large sequential databases such as online media library. The problem is concerned with efficiently locating subsequences referred to as queries in large archives of sequences or a single long sequence.

Pattern discovery: It aims to discover interesting patterns, which include periodic and abnormal patterns, from temporal data. The discovery of interesting patterns has become one of the most important data-mining tasks, and it can be applied to many domains. Particularly when the domain expert-derived patterns do not exist or are not complete, an algorithm to discover specific patterns or shapes automatically from the temporal data is necessary. Such an algorithm is noteworthy in that it does not assume prior knowledge of the number of interesting structures nor does it require an exhaustive explanation of the patterns being described.

2.5 SUMMARY

For temporal data mining, we presented three major phases of temporal data mining: representation of temporal data, definition of similarity measures, and mining tasks. Representation of temporal data refers to how to represent the temporal data in an efficient way before actually mining operations takes place. Three major methods including time domain–based representations, transformation-based representations, and generative model–based representations have been described and discussed in their advantages and disadvantages. In the transformation-based representations, four representations including PLS, PDWT, PCF, and DFT, which applied in our proposed algorithm—Weighted clustering ensemble with multiple representations presented in Chapter 7, have been described in detail. In generative model–based representations, HMM as an important model-based representation approach has been described with answering three questions related to its application of temporal data. After that, we described the similarity measures of temporal data mining based on different objectives: Similarity in time, similarity in shape, and similarity in change. For similarity in time, we described the Euclidean distance, which has been used for the similarity measure involved in our proposed algorithms that are Iteratively constructed clustering ensemble presented in Chapter 4 and Weighted clustering ensemble with multiple representations presented in Chapter 7, and explained how to apply such similarity measure on the different representations. For similarity in shapes, we described the DTW distance in detail. For similarity in change, a symmetric model–based distance measure and its variant named BP has been presented, and the KL distance which was used for our proposed *HMM-based meta clustering ensemble* presented in Chapter 5, has been further described here. After representing the temporal data in a suitable form, and defining the appropriate similarity measure, an algorithm would be used for a particular temporal data mining tasks, which is also called mining operation. Therefore, five mining tasks including prediction, classification, clustering, search & retrieval, and pattern discovery has been briefly described.

Temporal Data Clustering

3

CHAPTER OUTLINE

3.1 INTRODUCTION

Since temporal data have been dramatically increasing, temporal data mining has drawn much more attentions than ever. As one of important mining tasks, clustering provided underpinning techniques for discovering the intrinsic structure and condensing information over large amount of temporal data. In this chapter, we present a comprehensive survey on temporal data—clustering algorithms from different perspectives, which include partitional clustering, hierarchical clustering, density-based clustering, and model-based clustering. Their strengths and weakness are also discussed for temporal data clustering tasks. Moreover, based on the internal, external, and relative criteria, most common clustering validity indices are described for quantitative evaluation of clustering quality.

3.2 OVERVIEW OF CLUSTERING ALGORITHMS

Clustering can be considered the most important unsupervised learning problem: it deals with finding structure within a collection of unlabeled data. A cluster is therefore a collection of objects which are "similar" among themselves and "dissimilar" to objects belonging to other clusters. Data are called static if the feature values do not change, or change only negligibly, with time, and many clustering algorithms have been developed for static data-clustering analysis. Approached using different criteria, the taxonomies of static-clustering algorithms are many and various. However, a common framework (Jain et al., 1999) is still widely accepted for classifying clustering algorithms into partitioning clustering, hierarchical clustering, density-based clustering, and model-based clustering.

Although various algorithms have been developed to cluster different types of temporal data, they all try to modify the existing algorithms for clustering static data. This is done in such a way that temporal data can be handled or converted into the form of static data, meaning that existing algorithms for clustering static data can be directly applied. The former approach usually works directly with raw temporal data and is thus called the proximity-based approach. The major modification lies in replacing the distance/similarity measure for static data with one appropriate to temporal data. The latter approach first converts raw temporal data into either a feature vector with lower dimensions or a number of model parameters. It then applies a conventional clustering algorithm to the extracted feature vectors or model parameters. These are called the feature-based and model-based approaches, respectively. Three categorized temporal data clustering approaches are summarized in Table 3.1.

3.2.1 PARTITIONAL CLUSTERING

Partitioning clustering directly divides the data sets into several subsets, where each subset represents a cluster containing at least one data. In general, the partition is hard or crisp if each data belong to exactly one cluster or soft or fuzzy if one data are allowed to be in more than one cluster at a different degree, where each cluster is represented by a prototype and assigns the patterns to clusters according to most similar prototype. K-means algorithm (Forgy, 1965) and its modified version of K-medoids algorithm (Kaufman and Rousseeuw, 1990) are quite

Table 3.1 A Taxonomy on Temporal Data Clustering Algorithms

Methodology	Model-Based Clustering	Proximity-Based Clustering	Feature-Based Clustering
Working mechanism	• Clusters of temporal data are specified by a mixture of dynamic models • Identify the data dependency and regularity behind the dynamic behaviors of temporal data	• Works directly on temporal data • Similarity measure considering temporal relations	• A set of features are extracted from raw temporal data • All existing clustering algorithms can be applied directly on the feature space
Advantage	• Generally suitable for coping with data dependency among temporal data • Temporal data characterized with generative models	• Prevents loss of any information • A direct way to capture the dynamic behaviors • Flexible means to deal with variable length of temporal data	• Significantly reduces the computational cost • Compatible with existing static data clustering algorithms
Disadvantage	• Model selection problem • High computational complexity	• Sensitive to initialization • Model selection problem • High computational complexity	• Loss of useful information conveyed in the original temporal data • Model selection problem
Example	Hidden Markov Model—HMM (Smyth, 1999), dynamic Bayesian networks (Murphy, 2002), autoregressive moving average model (ARMA) (Xiong and Yeung, 2002)	Dynamic time warping—DTW (Keogh and Kasetty, 2003), temporal K-mean/hierarchical (Jain et al., 1999; Xu and Wunsch, 2005)	Polynomial/spline curve fitting (Liu and Brown, 2004), adaptive piecewise constant approximation (Sahouria and Zakhor, 1997), curvature-based PCA segments (Cheong et al., 2005), multiple-scaled i-k mean (Lin et al., 2004)

popular partitional-clustering algorithms, where each cluster is represented by either the mean value of the data points in the cluster or the most centrally located data points in a cluster. Two counterparts for fuzzy partitions are the fuzzy c-means algorithm (Bezdek, 1981; Hoeppner, 1999) and the fuzzy c-medoids algorithm (Krishnapuram et al., 2001). Actually there are many possible outputs obtained by partitioning the data sets into several groups, partitional-clustering algorithms always attempt to achieve a desired result by optimizing a criterion function such as square error, which is defined either globally or locally. These heuristic algorithms work well for finding spherical-shaped clusters and small to medium data sets, but they always reveal the weakness of analyzing the complex structured data such as temporal data.

K-means

It is one of the simplest partitional clustering algorithms and commonly used for solving temporal data clustering problem, for example, Liao et al. (2002) directly applied K-means as a proximity-based approach to multivariate battle simulation temporal data with the objective to form a discrete number of battle states or Vlachos et al. (2003) indirectly applied K-means as feature-based approach for analyzing time series on the wavelet-based representation. The procedure of K-means follows a simple way to classify a given temporal data set with a pre-defined number of clusters (assume K clusters), which it consists of the following steps:

1. Place K seed points into the representation space obtained from the data sets that are being clustered. These points represent initial groups.
2. Assign each data point to the group that has the closest seed point.
3. When all data points have been assigned, recalculate the positions of the K seed points.
4. Repeat steps 2 and 3 until the seed points no longer move. This produces a separation of the entire data set into groups known as clusters.

The entire process can be formulated by minimizing an objective function

$$\sum_{k=1}^{K} \sum_{x \in C_k} D(x, C_k) \tag{3.1}$$

where D is distance metric based on the meaningful objective (described in Section 2.3) to compute the distance between a data point x belonging to cluster k and representative point of the cluster C_k such as center of clustered data points.

Although the K-means can be proved that the learning procedure will always terminate at certain point, this algorithm does not necessarily find the most optimal solution, corresponding to the local minimum of objective function and sensitivity to the initialization and selection of number of seed points. Moreover, by directly applying K-means, it requires the temporal data with equal length because the concept of cluster centers would be ill defined when the individual one is represented in arbitrary length in the target data set.

Hidden Markov Model-Based K-Models Clustering

Essentially, Hidden Markov Model (HMM)-based K-models clustering is a K-means algorithm based on generative model—based representation, which has been commonly used for time series clustering task (Smyth, 1997; Zhong and Ghosh, 2003; Frossyniotis et al., 2004; Panuccio et al., 2009) due to its outstanding ability of capturing the dynamic behavior of time series. For partitional clustering, the entire data set $X = \{x_1, x_2, ...x_N\}$ is represented as a set of K HMM $\{\lambda_1, \lambda_2, ...\lambda_K\}$ with M states. As mentioned in Section 2.2.3, the emission probability function is defined as a single Gaussian distribution for the HMM-based K-models clustering implemented in our simulations. HMM model would consist of the parameters $\lambda = \{\pi, A, B\}$, where $\pi = \{\pi_j\}$, $A = \{a_{ij}\}$, $B = \left\{\mu_j, \sigma_j^2\right\}$. Therefore, the entire process of the algorithm aims to estimate the optimal parameters of components models with maximum log-likelihood.

Given the number of clusters K and the similarity measure based on model-based distance metric such as log-likelihood, the procedure of HMM-based K-models follows these steps:

1. Randomly select K items for data sets without replacements.
2. Initialize K HMM with predefined number of states M, and estimate the parameters of each HMM on one of selected items by expectation-maximization (EM) algorithm.
3. Compute log-likelihood of each item under K HMM by the forward and backward algorithms.
4. Assign each time to the HMM with maximum log-likelihood.
5. Re-estimate the parameters of K HMM on the corresponding cluster of item by EM algorithm.
6. Repeat steps 3 to 5 until the cluster memberships no longer change.

Although HMM-based K-models are a simple and efficient approach that solve temporal data clustering problems, this algorithm does not necessarily find the most optimal model configurations and is also quite sensitive to the initialization and selection of seed points number.

3.2.2 HIERARCHICAL CLUSTERING

Also known as a tree of clusters or a dendrogram, hierarchical clustering (Johnson, 1967) builds a cluster hierarchy in which every cluster node contains child clusters. These sibling clusters separate the points covered by their common parent allowing for the exploration of temporal data on different levels of granularity. In the early work (Van Wijk and Van Selow, 1999), they just performed an agglomerative hierarchical clustering of daily power consumption data based on the root mean-square distance. Hierarchical clustering methods are generally categorized as either agglomerative (bottom-up) or divisive (top-down). Agglomerative clustering begins with one-point (singleton) clusters and recursively merges two or more appropriate clusters. Divisive clustering begins with one cluster of all data points and recursively splits the most appropriate cluster. The process continues until a stopping criterion (frequently, the requested number K of clusters) is achieved. Theoretically, divisive hierarchical clustering is unfeasible because the possible divisions of data into two clusters at the first step of the algorithm are quite various. Therefore, in most applications, divisive hierarchical clustering is rarely applied which generally restricts attention to agglomerative hierarchical clustering.

Single Linkage

The simplest agglomerative hierarchical clustering approach is single linkage or the "nearest neighbor" technique. Key to this method is that the distance between groups is defined as the distance between the closest pair of objects came from different groups. In the single-linkage method,

$$D(R, S) = \min(D(r_i, s_j)) \qquad (3.2)$$

where object r_i is in cluster R and object s_j is in cluster S. The distance between every possible object pair (r_i, s_j) is computed, The minimum value of these distances is said to be the distance between clusters R and S. In other words, the distance between two clusters is given by the value of the shortest link between the clusters. At each stage of hierarchical clustering, the clusters R and S, for which $D(R, S)$ is minimum, are merged.

The single-linkage method works well on data sets containing nonisotropic clusters including well-separated, chain-like, and concentric clusters. Additionally, this method may be useful for the detection of outliers in the data set.

Complete Linkage

Complete linkage, or the "farthest neighbor" technique, is the opposite of single-linkage technique defining the distance between groups as the distance between the most distant pair of objects, one from each group. In the complete linkage method:

$$D(R, S) = \max(D(r_i, s_j)) \qquad (3.3)$$

where object r_i is in cluster R and object s_j is in cluster S. The distance between every possible object pair (r_i, s_j) is computed. The maximum value of these distances is said to be the distance between clusters R and S. In other words, the distance between two clusters is given by the value of the longest link between the clusters. At each stage of hierarchical clustering, the clusters R and S, for which $D(R, S)$ is minimum, are merged.

The complete linkage method produces a clustering result with smaller, tighter, and more compact clusters. Most of time, it is difficult to deal with complex cluster structures, and may gives a poor clustering result for temporal data.

Average Linkage

Here, the distance between two clusters is defined as the average of distances between all pairs of objects, where each pair is made up of one object from each group. In the average linkage method:

$$D(R, S) = T_{RS}/(N_R * N_S) \qquad (3.4)$$

where T_{RS} is the sum of all pairwise distances between cluster R and cluster S. N_R and N_S are the sizes of the clusters R and S, respectively. At each stage of hierarchical clustering, the clusters R and S, for which $D(R,S)$ is the minimum, are merged.

The average linkage method is a compromise between the single and complete linkage methods, which avoids the extremes of either large or tight compact clusters. Unlike other methods, the average linkage method has better performance on ball-shaped clusters in the feature space.

In general, the performance of an agglomerative hierarchical clustering method often suffers from its inability to adjust, once a merge decision has been executed. The same is true for divisive hierarchical clustering methods. Hierarchical clustering is not restricted to cluster time series with equal length. It is applicable to temporal data of unequal length as well if an appropriate distance measure such as dynamic time warping is used to compute the distance/similarity.

HMM-Based Agglomerative Clustering

HMM-based hierarchical agglomerative clustering was originally proposed by Smyth (1997). Initially, the N singleton HMM $\{\lambda_1, \lambda_2, ...\lambda_N\}$ is created and trained on each of items. Then the "closest" pair of clusters is recursively merged. It is quite important to choose the distance measure between the two clusters or models for hierarchical clustering. Conventional mergence of the two closest clusters (models) results in the largest log-likelihood $\log p(X|\lambda)$ (Ward, 1963; Fraley, 1999). Therefore, the distance can be defined as,

$$D(\lambda_i, \lambda_j) = \log p(X|\lambda_{before}) - \log p(X|\lambda_{after}) \tag{3.5}$$

where λ_{before} and λ_{after} are the entire set of parameters before and after merging two models (λ_i and λ_j), respectively.

However, this traditional model-based distance measure for model-based clustering is inefficient due to the fact of searching the closest pair of clusters needs to train the merged model for every pair and evaluate the resulting log-likelihood. Therefore, the Kullback-Leibler (KL) distance measure described in Section 2.3.3 is used for the single linkage, complete linkage, and average linkage methods of HMM-based hierarchical clustering. Although hierarchical agglomerative clustering avoids the problem of initialization, the distance comparison, mergence, and model estimation require high computation cost for temporal data clustering.

HMM-Based Divisive Clustering

HMM-based divisive clustering (Butler, 2003) is a "reverse" approach of HMM-agglomerative clustering, starting with one cluster or model of all data points and recursively splitting the most appropriate cluster. The process continues until a stopping criterion (pre-defined number K of clusters or models) is achieved. Initially, an HMM is trained on the whole data set. During each iteration of division, the "poorest-fit" cluster whose HMM gives the lowest likelihood to the items in this cluster would be split. This process is repeated until a stop criterion is reached or all the clusters become singletons.

Like HMM-based agglomerative clustering, this still suffers from high computational costs and model selection problems. Moreover, it is quite sensitive to initialization, due to the possible divisions of data into two clusters at the first step.

3.2.3 DENSITY-BASED CLUSTERING

Density-based clustering algorithms are designed to find the arbitrary-shaped clusters in data sets, a cluster is defined as a high-density region, which exceeds a threshold, separated by low-density regions in data space. Density-Based Spatial Clustering of Applications with Noise, DBSCAN (Ester et al., 1996) is a typical density-based clustering algorithm. The basic idea of DBSCAN is to iteratively grow a cluster of data points as long as the density in the "neighborhood" exceeds some threshold. Rather than producing a clustering explicitly, Ordering Points To Identify the Clustering Structure (Ankerst et al., 1999) computes an augmented cluster ordering for automatic and interactive cluster analysis. The ordering contains information that is equivalent to density-based clustering obtained from a wide range of parameter settings, thus overcoming the difficulty of selecting parameter values. For analyzing time series—contained significant noise, density-based clustering has been typically applied by Denton (2005) to identify and remove this noise by only considering clusters rising above a preset threshold in the density landscape, while Jiang et al. (2003) proposed a density-based hierarchical clustering to tackle the problem of effectively clustering time series gene expression data, where all objects in a data set are organized into an attraction tree according to the density-based connectivity, the clusters are then identified by dense areas.

Density-Based Spatial Clustering of Applications with Noise

The basic idea of DBSCAN is to iteratively construct a new cluster from a selected data point by absorbing all data points in its neighborhood. It is based on two main concepts: density reachability and density connectability (Ester et al., 1996). Both of these concepts depend on two input parameters of the DBSCAN clustering: the size of neighborhood ε defined as a semidiameter of neighborhood based on Euclidean distance and the minimum number of data points in a cluster N^{minPts}. The entire process of DBSCAN involves the following steps:

1. It starts with an arbitrary starting point that has not been visited. It then finds all the neighbor points within distance ε from the starting point.
2. If the number of neighbors is greater than or equal to N^{minPts}, a cluster is formed. The starting point called core point and its neighbors are added to this cluster, and the starting point is marked as visited. Otherwise the point is marked as noise.
3. For each neighbor of core points in the current cluster, it is to mark it as visited. If the number of its neighbors is greater than or equal to N^{minPts} and its neighbors which are not already contained in the current cluster are added to the current cluster, this process continues until the cluster cannot be expanded.

4. Then the algorithm proceeds to iterate through the remaining unvisited points in the data set.

In general, DBSCAN is beneficial from automatically detecting the number of clusters, ability to find arbitrarily shaped clusters, and relatively insensitive to noise and ordering of points in the database. However, it has the limitation to dealing with the high-dimensional data such as time series and has a difficulty to cluster data sets with large differences in densities.

3.2.4 MODEL-BASED CLUSTERING

In model-based clustering, we use certain models for describing groups of data points, and each cluster can be mathematically represented by a parametric model, such as HMM or autoregressive moving average model. The entire data set is therefore modeled by a mixture of these component models. An component model is used to represent a specific cluster that is often referred to a probability distribution. A large amount of literature (Picone, 1990; Smyth, 1997; Beran and Mazzola, 1999; Oates et al., 1999; Fraley and Raftery, 2002; Ramoni et al., 2002; Xiong and Yeung, 2002; Bagnall and Janacek, 2004; Pavlovic, 2004; Panuccio et al., 2009) have shown that the model-based approaches have been widely used for time series clustering analysis.

For a data set of N objects $x = \{x_n\}_{n=1}^{N}$, a mixture of models is defined as a linear combination of K component distributions and formulated as,

$$p(x|\theta) = \sum_{k=1}^{K} w_k \, p(x|\theta_k) \tag{3.6}$$

where $\theta = \{\theta_k\}_{k=1}^{K}$ is the unknown model parameter, w_k is the prior probability (also known as mixing or weighting coefficient), and satisfies the requirements $0 \leq w_k \leq 1$, and $\sum_{k=1}^{K} w_k = 1$. K is the number of component models representing the entire data set. In the model-based clustering, finding the clusters of a given data set is equivalent to estimating the parameters θ_k of each component distribution. The maximum likelihood (ML) estimation (Bilmes, 1998) is a useful statistical approach for parameter estimation, which finds the optimal parameters by maximizing a likelihood function derived from the observed data.

$$p(\{x_1, \ldots, x_N\}|\theta) = \prod_{n=1}^{N} \left(\sum_{k=1}^{K} w_k \, p(x_n|\theta_k) \right) \tag{3.7}$$

or in a logarithm form

$$l(\theta) = \sum_{n=1}^{N} \log \left(\sum_{k=1}^{k} w_k \, p(x_n|\theta_k) \right) \tag{3.8}$$

However, the computation of maximizing the log-likelihood is quite complex in most circumstances. Therefore, a powerful technique called EM algorithm (Dempster et al., 1977; Bilmes, 1998; Fraley and Raftery, 2002) is introduced in order to optimize such computation involved.

EM Algorithm

The EM algorithm is an iterative approach for ML parameter estimation from the observable data $\{x_n\}$ as incomplete data. Then the cluster label $\{y_n\}$ would be treated as missing data. Both observable data $\{x_n\}$ and cluster label $\{y_n\}$ construct the complete data. Thus, the complete data log-likelihood is formulated as,

$$l(\theta) = \sum_{n=1}^{N} \sum_{k=1}^{k} p(y_n|x_n)\log(w_k p(x_n|\theta_k)) \tag{3.9}$$

The posterior probability $p(y_n|x_n)$ represents the probability that a component model generating the data point x_n is signed by label y_n, which is defined as

$$p(y_n|x_n) = \frac{w_{y_n} \, p(x_n|\theta_{y_n})}{\sum_k w_k \, p(x_n|\theta_k)} \tag{3.10}$$

In producing a series of parameter estimations $\theta^t = \{\theta^0, \theta^1, ..., \theta^T\}$ until the convergence criterion is met, EM algorithm iteratively invokes the following steps:

1. Initialize $\theta^0 = \{\theta_k^0\}_{k=1}^{K}$ and set $t = 0$.
2. E-step: estimation of the posterior probability of missing data.

$$p(y_n = k|x_n) = \frac{w_{y_n} \, p\left(x_n \middle| \theta_{y_n}^t\right)}{\sum_k w_k \, p(x_n|\theta_k)} \tag{3.11}$$

3. M-step: re-estimation of model parameters.

$$\theta_{y_n}^{t+1} = \arg\max_{\theta} \sum_{n=1}^{N} p(y_n|x_n)p(x_n|\theta) \tag{3.12}$$

For model-based clustering, EM algorithm has the advantage (Bilmes, 1998) of conceptual simplicity and ease of implementation of estimating the model parameters. It iteratively optimizes the log-likelihood-based objective function, and has good rate of convergence on the first few steps. However, this approach cannot always guarantee to provide the best solution, and sometimes converges to a local optima. Moreover, its process always becomes quite slow for dealing with the temporal data with large volume and high dimensionality.

HMM-Based Hybrid Partitional-Hierarchical Clustering

As mentioned in the early sections, both HMM-based K-models and HMM-based hierarchical clustering have their own characters. In order to combine the strengths of model-based partitional and hierarchical approaches, Zhong and Ghosh (2003) proposed an HMM-based hybrid partitioning-hierarchical clustering.

For the hybrid approach, the whole data set is initially partitioned into K_0 clusters (K_0 is greater than the intrinsic number of clusters K) by HMM-based K-models. Then the flat K_0 clusters are used as the input of HMM-based agglomerative clustering and the closed clusters based on a specified distance measure are iteratively merged until the stop criterion is reached. The entire procedure is presented by following steps:

1. Flat partitional clustering: partition data objects into K_0 clusters by using HMM-based K-models clustering.
2. Distance calculation: compute pairwise intercluster distances using distance measures based on log-likelihood and identify the closest cluster pair.
3. Cluster merging: merge the two closest clusters and re-estimate a model for the merged data objects.
4. Stop if all data objects have been merged into one cluster or if a user-specified number of clusters is reached. Otherwise, go back to second step.

Although the HMM-based hybrid partitional-hierarchical clustering is able to reduce complexity of applying agglomerative clustering by using a preprocess based on partitional clustering, this hybrid clustering approach still suffers from the initialization problem and model selection problem of detecting the intrinsic number of clusters.

HMM-Based Hierarchical Metaclustering

The HHM-based hierarchical metaclustering (Zhong and Ghosh, 2003) is a modified version of hybrid clustering described previously. It treats each initial cluster obtained from the flat partitional clustering as metadata and applies standard HMM-based agglomerative clustering to group the meta data. Therefore, the composite model $\lambda_{i,j}$ obtained from the pair of merged clusters λ_i and λ_j is defined as combined parameters of children $\lambda_{i,j} = \{\lambda_i, \lambda_j\}$, and the log-likelihood of the composite model on the data associated with both merged clusters is defined as $\log p\left(X_{i,j} \mid \lambda_{i,j}\right) = \log p(X_i \mid \lambda_i) + \log p(X_j \mid \lambda_j)$, where $X_{i,j} = X_i \cup X_j$. For agglomerative clustering based on the KL distance measure (e.g., *Min*KL, *Max*KL, *Boundary*KL) detailed in Section 2.3.3, the distance between two composite models is defined as $D(\lambda_a, \lambda_b) = D^{KL}_{\lambda \in \lambda_a \& \lambda' \in \lambda_b}(\lambda, \lambda')$, where $\lambda_a = \{\lambda_{a1}, \lambda_{a2}...\}$ *and* $\lambda_b = \{\lambda_{b1}, \lambda_{b2}...\}$. This approach is implemented as following steps:

1. Flat partitional clustering: partition data objects into K_0 clusters using one of the model-based partitional clustering algorithms such as HMM-based K-models clustering.

2. Distance calculation: compute pairwise intercluster distances using distance measures based on log-likelihood and identify the closest cluster pair,
3. Cluster merging: merge the two closest clusters to form a composite model $\lambda_{i,j} = \{\lambda_i, \lambda_j\}$. The distance between two composite models $\lambda_a = \{\lambda_{a1}, \lambda_{a2}...\}$ and $\lambda_b = \{\lambda_{b1}, \lambda_{b2}...\}$ is defined as KL distance measure $D(\lambda_a, \lambda_b) = D^{KL}_{\lambda \in \lambda_a \& \lambda' \in \lambda_b}(\lambda, \lambda')$.
4. Stop if all data objects have been merged into one cluster or if a user-specified number of clusters is reached. Otherwise, go back to second step.

In comparison with original version, this approach further reduces computational cost due to the fact of that no re-estimation of merged models is required and well captures the character of complex structure of cluster than single model that is difficult to define and train by using a composite model represented by the parameter of its children models. However, the initial clustering analysis still causes the initialization problem by using HMM-based K-models and also requires a predefined number of clusters as an important input to the algorithm.

3.3 CLUSTERING VALIDATION

How to evaluate clustering results obtained by different clustering algorithms is the main subject of clustering validation. For a 2-3D clustering output space, the clustering result can be evaluated by the subjective visual inspection, which is often difficult and expensive for a large multidimensional data set such as temporal data. Other solutions are concerned with the clustering validation technique based on two criteria (Halkidi et al., 2001), namely the compactness and separation of cluster membership. For compactness, the members of each cluster should be as close to each other as possible. For separation, the clusters should be widely placed.

In order to access clustering quality based on the two criteria mentioned previously, three groups of cluster validity indices (Dunn, 1974; Davies and Bouldin, 1979; Sharma, 1995; Halkidi et al., 2001; Halkidi and Vazirgiannis, 2001) have been developed for quantitative evaluation of the clustering results based on external, internal, and relative measures (Theodoridis et al., 1999), respectively. The external measures require the class label (ground truth) to be known, where the clustering result generated by a clustering algorithm is compared to the prespecified partition of a data set based on the ground truth or the proximity matrix is compared to the prespecified partition. The internal measures are to verify whether the cluster structure produced by a clustering algorithm fits the data set, by using only information inherent to the data set. Both external and internal validation methods are based on statistical tests requiring high computational costs. However, the principal idea of the third approach, based on the relative criteria, is to determine the best clustering results generated from the same clustering algorithm but with different parameterization.

3.3.1 **CLASSIFICATION ACCURACY**

Classification accuracy as the simplest clustering quality measure was proposed by Gavrilov et al. (2000) to evaluate clustering results associated with the ground truth. Given the partition of the data set based on the ground truth $P^* = \{C_1^*, \ldots C_K^*\}$ and clustering results generated by clustering algorithm $P = \{C_1, \ldots C_K\}$, the similarity between them is formulated as

$$CA(P^*, P) = \left(\sum_{i=1}^{K} \max_{j} Sim(C_i^*, C_j) \right) \Big/ K \qquad (3.13)$$

where $Sim(C_i^*, C_j) = 2\frac{|C_i^* \cap C_j|}{|C_i^*|+|C_j|}$ and K is the number of clusters.

3.3.2 **ADJUSTED RAND INDEX**

The Adjusted Rand Index (ARI) (Halkidi et al., 2002) is defined by

$$ARI(P^*, P) = \frac{\sum_{i,j}\binom{N_{ij}}{2} - \left[\sum_i\binom{N_i}{2}\sum_j\binom{N_j}{2}\right]\Big/\binom{N}{2}}{\frac{1}{2}\left[\sum_i\binom{N_i}{2} + \sum_j\binom{N_j}{2}\right] - \left[\sum_i\binom{N_i}{2}\sum_j\binom{N_j}{2}\right]\Big/\binom{N}{2}}. \qquad (3.14)$$

Here, N is the number of data points in a given data set and N_{ij} is the number of data points of the class label $C_j^* \in P^*$ assigned to cluster C_i in partition P. N_i is the number of data points in cluster C_i of partition P, and N_j is the number of data points in class C_j^*. In general, an ARI value lies between 0 and 1. The index value is equal to 1 only if a partition is completely identical to the intrinsic structure and close to 0 for a random partition.

3.3.3 **JACCARD INDEX**

The Jaccard Index (Halkidi et al., 2002), also known as the Jaccard similarity coefficient is defined by

$$J(P^*, P) = \frac{\sum_{i,j}\binom{N_{ij}}{2}}{\sum_i\binom{N_i}{2} + \sum_j\binom{N_j}{2} - \sum_i\binom{N_{ij}}{2}}. \qquad (3.15)$$

Here, N_{ij} is the number of data points of the class label $C_j^* \in P^*$ assigned to clusters C_i in partition P. N_i is the number of data points is in cluster C_i of partition P, and N_j is the number of data points in class C_j^*.

3.3.4 MODIFIED HUBERT'S Γ INDEX

Modified Hubert's Γ Index (MHΓ) (Theodoridis et al., 1999) is given by the following equation

$$MHT(P) = \frac{2}{N(N-1)} \sum_{i=1}^{N-1} \sum_{j=i+1}^{N} PM_{ij}Q_{ij} \tag{3.16}$$

where PM_{ij} is the proximity matrix, and Q is $N \times N$ cluster distance-based matrix based on partition P, where Q_{ij} is the distance between the centers of clusters to which x_i and x_j belong. In the MHΓ, the high value represents a compact and well-separated clustering structure of the partition.

3.3.5 DUNN'S VALIDITY INDEX

The Dunn's Validity Index (DVI) (Dunn, 1974) is given by the following equation

$$DVI\ (P) = \min_{i,j} \left\{ \frac{d(c_i, c_j)}{\max\limits_{k=1...K_m} \left\{ diam(c_k) \right\}} \right\} \tag{3.17}$$

where $[c_i, c_j, c_k] \in P$, $d(c_i, c_j)$ is the single-linkage dissimilarity function between two clusters and $diam(c_k)$ is the diameter of cluster, c_k, based on assessed partition, P. Similar to the MHΓ, DVI also assesses the clustering quality based on compactness and separation of clusters in the partition.

3.3.6 DAVIES-BOULDIN VALIDITY INDEX

The Davis-Bouldin Validity index (Davies and Bouldin, 1979) is a function of the ratio of the sum of within-cluster scatter and between-cluster separation

$$DB(P) = \frac{1}{K} \sum_{i,j=1}^{K} \max_{i \neq j} \left\{ \frac{Dist(Q_i) + Dist(Q_j)}{Dist(Q_i, Q_j)} \right\} \tag{3.18}$$

where K is the number of clusters. $Dist(Q_i)$ is the average distance of all objects from the cluster to their cluster center Q_i in partition PP and $Dist(Q_i, Q_j)$ is the distance between cluster centers (Q_i, Q_j). Hence, the ratio is small if the clusters are compact and far from each other. Consequently, the Davies-Bouldin index will have a small value for good clustering.

3.3.7 NORMALIZED MUTUAL INFORMATION

Normalized mutual information (NMI) (Vinh et al., 2009) is proposed to measure the consistency between any two partitions, which indicates the amount of information (common structured objects) shared between two partitions. Given a set of partitions $\{P_t\}_{t=1}^{T}$ obtained from a target data set, the NMI-based clustering validity criteria of assessed partition P_a are determined by summation of the NMI between the assessed partition P_a and each individual partition P_m. Therefore, the high-valued NMI represents a well-accepted partition and indicates the intrinsic structure of the target data set. However, this approach always shows bias toward highly correlated partitions and favors the balanced structure of the data set. The NMI is calculated as following

$$NMI(P_a, P_b) = \frac{\sum_{i=1}^{K_a} \sum_{j=1}^{K_b} N_{ij}^{ab} \log\left(\frac{NN_{ij}^{ab}}{N_i^a N_j^b}\right)}{\sum_{i=1}^{K_a} N_i^a \log\left(\frac{N_i^a}{N}\right) + \sum_{j=1}^{K_b} N_j^b \log\left(\frac{N_j^b}{N}\right)} \qquad (3.19)$$

$$NMI(P) = \sum_{t=1}^{T} NMI(P, P_t) \qquad (3.20)$$

Here P_a and P_b are labelings for two partitions that divide a data set of N objects into K_a and K_b clusters, respectively. N_{ij}^{ab} is the number of shared objects between clusters $C_i^a \in P_a$ and $C_j^b \in P_b$, where there are N_i^a and N_j^b objects in C_i^a and C_j^b.

3.4 SUMMARY

Temporal data clustering is to partition an unlabeled temporal data set into groups or clusters, where all the sequences grouped in the same cluster should be coherent or homogeneous. Although various algorithms have been developed to cluster different types of temporal data, they all try to modify the existing clustering algorithms for processing temporal information.

Such approaches usually work directly with raw temporal data and are thus called the proximity-based approach. The major modification lies in the fact that the distance/similarity measure for static data is replaced by the one appropriate to temporal data. By directly applying the clustering algorithms to temporal data, most partitioning clustering suffer from model-selection problems and sensitivity to initialization, and hierarchical clustering has difficulties in properly grouping temporal data with high dimensionality. Density-based clustering is beneficial from automatically detecting the number of clusters, and in turn finding arbitrarily shaped clusters, but it still has the limitation of dealing with temporal data with high dimensionality and large differences in densities.

In contrast, other approaches are to convert the raw temporal data into either a number of statistical models or a feature vector with lower dimensions firstly and then apply a conventional clustering algorithm to the representative models or extracted feature vectors. These methods are often called the model-based and feature-based approaches. Although model-based clustering algorithms are able to model the dynamic behaviors of temporal data, there are also several drawbacks such as computational costs and sensitivity to model configuration, which critically determines its performance. By indirectly applying the clustering algorithms to temporal data based on their representations, feature extraction as a vital process in feature-based clustering algorithms will always imperfectly represent all differently structured temporal data as each feature extraction accommodates a limited amount of characters obtained from temporal data. Therefore, we cannot solely rely on these algorithms for robust clustering analysis on temporal data. This, in turn, means that another advanced technique, the ensemble learning described in the later chapter, is required to improve the performance of temporal data clustering.

At the end of the chapter, most common clustering validity indices are described for quantitative evaluation of clustering quality based on the internal, external, and relative criteria. In addition, three clustering validity indices, including MHΓ, DVI, and NMI detailed in this chapter, would be used to constitute the basic concept of a partition weighting scheme for the proposed Weighted clustering ensemble with multiple representations presented in Chapter 7.

Ensemble Learning

4

CHAPTER OUTLINE

4.1 INTRODUCTION

Ensemble learning was originally proposed for classification tasks in a manner of supervised learning in 1965 (Nilsson, 1965); the basic concept of ensemble learning is to train multiple base learners as ensemble members and combine their predictions into a single output that should have better performance on average than any other ensemble member with uncorrelated error on the target data sets. For classification tasks, many researchers have demonstrated the outstanding performance of ensemble learning in their works (Wittner and Denker, 1988; Ho et al., 1994; Cho and Kim, 1995; Breiman, 1996a,b; Raftery et al., 1997; Kittler et al., 1998; Schapire, 1999; Jain et al., 2000; Oza and Tumer, 2001; Tumer and Oza, 2003). Although all these approaches are proposed from various perspectives, they all have to address the fundamental problems of ensemble learning: how to train each of base learners (Ensemble learning algorithms), how to combine the outputs obtained from the multiple base learners (combining methods), and what is the critical factor to determine the success of ensemble learning (ensemble diversity). In this chapter, we are going to answer these questions.

Recently, ensemble learning has been extended to unsupervised learning with different strategies, named as clustering ensemble. This has led to many real-world applications, such as gene classification, image segmentation, video retrieval, and so on.

In this chapter, we are going to describe a general framework of clustering ensemble with two major functions including consensus function and objective function.

4.2 ENSEMBLE LEARNING ALGORITHMS

In ensemble learning approach, the multiple base learner can be trained either co-ordinately in a sequential manner or individually in a parallel manner. Although many ensemble learning approaches are designed by following these training processes, we are typically going to review two of the most attentional algorithms, which give the initial inspiration to propose the *Iteratively constructed clustering ensemble* model presented in Chapter 6.

Bagging

It is the simplest and most appealing sampling-based ensemble approach. Originally, introduced by Breiman (1996a,b) for supervised learning, this idea has recently been extended to clustering tasks (Dudoit and Fridlyand, 2003; Fischer and Buhmann, 2003). In essence, bagging generates multiple ensemble members built on a bootstrap with replicates of the training set. Then, these ensemble members are combined into the final output by majority voting. The literature (Breiman, 1996a,b) shows us that the performance of a ensemble approach often depends on the diversity of ensemble members in the combination. The sampling procedure of bagging simply creates various training samples from the training set by bootstrap sampling, resulting in diversity among the ensemble members. The ensemble output is then able to reduce the bias and variability, for example, the sensitivity to starting conditions and the possibility of convergence to local minima, in the classification results via the averaging procedure of majority voting. The process of bagging involves following the steps:

1. Create a training set with replacement by randomly sampling the data sets
2. Train the base learner on the training set
3. Repeat 1—2 until satisfying the stopping criteria, for example, the maximum number of loop reached
4. A final classifier is formed by aggregating the trained base learners
5. A testing set can be classified by a majority voting under the final classifier

Boosting

Boosting was originally started from an online learning algorithm named Adaboost (Freund and Schapire, 1997). It sequentially build up a linear combination of base learners that concentrate on difficult examples, such approach results in great success in supervised learning. Recent work (Frossyniotis et al., 2004; Pavlovic, 2004; Liu et al., 2007; Saffari and Bischof, 2007) has extended it with unsupervised learning manner with different strategies. The basic idea of boosting clustering is that each training instance is assigned an adapted weight that determines how "good" the instance was when classified in the previous iteration. Subsets of training data with high (badly clustered) value are more likely to be trained during each iteration, it means paying more attention to instances which are difficult to classify. Clearly, a boosting ensemble is based on sequential runs with pertinent feedback from previous trained base learner. This is different from parallel approaches such as bagging. A general procedure of boosting algorithm follows these steps:

1. Initialize the weights of instances in the data set as $1/N$ (N is the number of instances in the data set)
2. Create a training set by sampling the data set based on the instance weights, where the instances with higher weights are more likely to be selected
3. Train the base learner on the training set, and compute the training error
4. Based on the training error, compute the weight of current trained base learner, and update the weights of instances
5. Repeat steps 1−2 until satisfying the stopping criteria, for example, the maximum number of loops reached or the training error exceeds a threshold
6. A final classifier is form by aggregating the trained base learners associated with their weights
7. A testing set can be classified by a weighted majority voting under the final classifier

4.3 COMBINING METHODS

As long as the multiple base learners have been trained, ensemble learning algorithms have to employ an appropriate method as a combiner to combine their training outputs into a single form as final classifier. Although there are a large number of combining methods appeared in the literature, three of them have been most commonly used and demonstrated good performance for a numerous applications of ensemble learning, which are linear combiner, product combiner, and majority voting combiner (Brown, 2009).

Linear Combiner

In ensemble learning algorithms, a linear combiner is specially applied for supervised learning tasks including classification and regression, where the outputs of the trained base learner are real-valued probability estimates of class label given the input data. Therefore, the combination of these base learners can be formulated as an ensemble probability estimate:

$$p(y|x) = \sum_{t=1}^{T} w_t p_t(y|x) \tag{4.1}$$

where $p_t(y|x)$ is the probability of estimating the class label y given the input data x by the trained base learner t and assigned a weight w_t to determine its performance based on the training set. If the weights of the trained base learners are uniformly distributed $w_t = 1/T$, $\forall t$, the probability estimates of the trained base learners are uniformly averaged into the ensemble probability estimate. Otherwise, the ensemble probability estimate is a weighted average of the probability estimates of the trained base learners. In general, a linear combiner based on weighted average provides a more meaningful combination of base learners and achieves the better performance than the linear combiner based on uniform average.

Product Combiner

If the base learners are trained on the feature spaces, where training sets are highly corrected, the linear combination rule is able to achieve the optimal performance of ensemble learning. However, when the base learner is trained on independent feature spaces, where training sets are uncorrected, it is efficient to combine the trained base learners by multiplying their real-valued probabilistic outputs, which can be formulated as a product combiner:

$$p(y|x) = \frac{1}{Z} \prod_{t}^{T} p_t(y|x) \tag{4.2}$$

where Z is constant-valued factor to normalize the ensemble probability estimate into a valid distribution.

Majority Voting Combiner

Actually both linear and product combination rules are employed for the real-value outputs obtained from the trained base learners. If the base learners directly estimate the class label given the input data, a majority voting combiner can be used to decide the class label of the input data by counting the votes among all trained base learners, which is formulated as:

$$H^i = \arg\max_{j} \sum_{t}^{T} w_t H_t^{i,j} \tag{4.3}$$

where $H_t^{i,j} = \begin{cases} 1 & \textit{if data i is assigned to class j} \\ 0 & \textit{Otherwise} \end{cases}$ in partition t. If the weights of the trained base learners are uniformly distributed $w_t = 1/T$, $\forall t$, a simple majority voting combiner is formed and commonly used for bagging. Otherwise, a weighted majority voting can be used for boosting.

4.4 DIVERSITY OF ENSEMBLE LEARNING

If a single classification solution does not make any error, the ensemble is unnecessary. If, however, the classification solution does make errors, we seek to complement it with another ensemble member, which makes errors on different objects. Therefore, we realize that the diversity of the ensemble members/trained base learners would therefore be a critical requirement for the success of the ensemble learning. Although many diversity measures have been designed to qualify the diversity of ensemble members, they are generally classified into two categories including pairwise measures and nonpairwise measures. Pairwise measures consider difference between a pair of ensemble members at a time; the overall differences as ensemble diversity value is obtained by averaging across all pairs, for example, *Disagreement measure* (Skalak, 1996) and *Double-fault measure* (Giacinto and Roli, 2001). In contrast, nonpairwise measures consider all the ensemble members together and calculate directly one diversity value for the ensemble, for example, *Entropy measure* (Cunningham and Carney, 2000), *Kohavi-Wolpert variance* (Kohavi and Wolpert, 1996), *The measure of difficulty* (Hansen and Salamon, 1990), *Measurement of inter-rater agreement* (Fleiss, 1973), and *Generalized diversity* (Partridge and Krzanowski, 1997).

In general, diversity alone is not to be beneficial to the ensemble performance, the trained base learners have to be at the same time accurate and diverse in order to produce an optimal ensemble output. Moreover, it is difficult to determine a generally accepted definition of ensemble diversity and even more difficult to relate that measure to the ensemble performance in a neat and expressive dependency. However, it practically provides a guideline for the design of ensemble learning models with better performance. Normally, an ensemble learning algorithm can be designed in one of the three ways:

1. Combining the different base learners trained on the same training set into a final ensemble output such as random subspace (Ho, 1998)
2. Combining the same base learners trained on the different training sets into a final ensemble output by applying a resampling technique on the entire data set such as bagging (Breiman, 1996a,b) and boosting (Freund and Schapire, 1997)
3. Combining the same base learners trained with different parameters and initialization into a final ensemble output such as neural network ensemble (Sharkey, 1999)

4.5 CLUSTERING ENSEMBLE

As described in Section 3.2, it is obvious that each clustering algorithm behaves differently and with its own characteristics. No single clustering algorithm is able to achieve satisfactory results for all types of data set. From the perspective of machine learning, clustering analysis is also an extremely difficult unsupervised learning task since it is inherently an ill-posed problem with solutions which often violate some common assumptions (Kleinberg, 2003). However, there are many feasible approaches developed to improve the performance of clustering analysis. Among them is the ensemble learning method.

Although ensemble method has become an active research area in supervised learning domain and provides a popular way to improve the performance of classification task, it is still quite difficult to directly apply such ideas to unsupervised domain (clustering ensemble) due to two major issues:

1. Unlike classification ensemble, it is not possible to precisely evaluate the quality of different ensemble members (clustering results) for clustering ensemble without providing the priori labeling information of training data. Therefore, the idea of classification ensemble such as boosting cannot be directly applied for clustering task.

2. Unlike classification ensemble, it cannot immediately determine which cluster from one particular clustering result corresponds to which in an other result for clustering ensemble, where different partitions produce incompatible labeling information, resulting in intractable correspondence problems, especially when the numbers of clusters are different. Therefore, directly combining the clustering results with the combination rules (linear combiner, product combiner, and majority voting combiner) becomes meaningless for clustering task.

Recently, clustering ensemble techniques have been studied from different perspectives, for example, clustering ensembles with graph partitioning (Karypis and Kumar, 1999; Strehl and Ghosh, 2003; Fern and Brodley, 2004; Analoui and Sadighian, 2007) evidence aggregation (Monti et al., 2003; Fred and Jain, 2005; Gionis et al., 2007; Ailon et al., 2008; Yang and Chen, 2011a,b) and optimization via semidefinite programming (Singh et al., 2007). The basic idea underlying clustering ensemble techniques is the combining of multiple partitions of a data set by a consensus function yielding a final partition that more likely reflects the intrinsic structure of the data set. Due to the nature of combining the strengths of multiple clustering solutions, clustering ensembles generally outperform the single clustering from several aspects including robustness, novelty, stability, confidence estimation, parallelization, and scalability (Ghaemi et al., 2009).

4.5.1 CONSENSUS FUNCTIONS

The core of a clustering ensemble is the consensus function which must address three issues: how to combine different clustering solutions, how to overcome the label corresponding problem, and how to ensure symmetrical and unbiased consensus with respect to all the input partitions. Many approaches have been developed to solve consensus clustering problems. Ghaemi et al. (2009) have summarized the consensus functions shown in Table 4.1, where K is the number of clusters, N is the size of data set/number of objects, T is the number of ensemble members/input partitions, I is the number of iterations to reach convergence, d is the number of dimension in original feature space, and d' is the number of dimension in transformed feature space. Based on the comparison of their advantages, disadvantages, and computational complexity, we release all the approaches that are able to produce a robust consensus clustering result but most just obtain a trade-off solution between computational cost and accuracy.

Table 4.1 Summarized Consensus Functions

Algorithm	Advantages	Disadvantages	Computing Complexity
METIS (Karypis and Kumar, 1999)	• Coarsens the graph by collapsing vertices and edges • Partitions the coarsened graph and refines the partitions	• Compared to HBGF, low robust clustering performance of METIS • High computational cost	$O(KNT)$
SPEC (Ng et al., 2001)	• A popular multiway spectral graph partitioning algorithm (SPEC) that seeks to optimize the normalized cut criterion	• Compared to HBGF, low robust clustering performance of SPEC • High computational cost	$O(N^3)$
CSPA HGPA MCLA (Strehl and Ghosh, 2003)	• Knowledge reuse; to influence a new cluster based on a different set of features • Controls size of partitions • Low computational cost of HGPA • Improves the quality and robustness of the solution • Allows one to add a stage that selects the best consensus function without any supervisory information by objective function	• High computational cost of CSPA and MCLA • The proposed greedy approach is slowest and is often intractable for large data sets	CSPA-$O(KN^2T)$ HGPA-$O(KNT)$ MCLA-$O(K^2NT^2)$
HBGF (Fern and Brodley, 2004)	• Low computational cost • High robust clustering performance against instance-based and cluster-based approaches • Compared to IBGF and CBGF, the reduction of HBGF is negligible	• Retains all the information of an ensemble • Difficult implementation	$O(KN)$

Continued

Table 4.1 Summarized Consensus Functions—cont'd

Algorithm	Advantages	Disadvantages	Computing Complexity
PBC (Fischer and Buhmann, 2003)	• Extracting arbitrary shaped structures from the data • Automatic outlier detection • Avoiding the dependency on small fluctuations in the data • High stability	• Requires a very high volume of clustering to obtain a reliable result • High computational cost	$O(K^3)$
BagClust (Dudoit and Fridlyand, 2003)	• Reduces variability in the partitioning results via averaging • Improves clustering accuracy by using bagging to cluster analysis • More robust to the variable selection scheme by bagged clustering procedures	• The increase in accuracy observed with PAM is due to a decrease in variability achieved by aggregating multiple clustering • High computational cost	$O(K^3)$
CMWC (Topchy et al., 2003)	• Uses two different weak clustering algorithms: clustering of multidimensional data; clustering by splitting the data using a number of random hyperplanes • Low computational cost	• Requires a few restarts in order to avoid convergence to low-quality local minima	$O(KNT)$
CMCITG (Luo et al., 2006)	• Uses a consensus scheme via the genetic algorithm • Improves accuracy and robustness	• High computational cost	$O(K^3)$
NEACE (Azimi et al., 2007)	• Generates a new feature space from initial clustering outputs better than pure or normalized feature space • Uses a modification of k means for initial clustering named intelligent k-means • Fast convergence • Low computational cost	• Difficult implementation • Unsuitable accuracy	$O(K! + KTldd')$

Table 4.1 Summarized Consensus Functions—cont'd

Algorithm	Advantages	Disadvantages	Computing Complexity
VKM (Fred, 2001)	• Uses a minimum spanning tree for consistent cluster development • Handles the problem of initialization dependency and selection of the number of clusters by voting-k-means algorithm • Does not entail any specificity toward a particular clustering strategy by the proposed technique	• Does not correspond to known number of classes with number of concluded clusters • High computational cost • Fixed threshold	$O(N^2)$
ClusterFusion (Kellam et al., 2001)	• Uses a comparison metric known as weighted kappa and finds known biological relationships among genes • Generates robust clusters	• Difficult implementation • High computational cost	$O(N^2)$
DCUEA (Fred and Jain, 2005)	• Applies a minimum spanning tree (MST)-based clustering algorithm on a coassociation matrix based on a voting mechanism • The ability of the proposed method to identify arbitrary shaped clusters in multidimensional data	• High computational cost • Poor performance of method in situations involving touching clusters	$O(N^2)$
ACE (Topchy et al., 2004)	• Uses a finite mixture of multinominal distributions in the space of cluster labels • Excellent scalability of algorithm • Comprehensible underlying model • Completely avoids having to solve the label correspondence problem	• High computational cost for minimal weight bipartite matching problem	$O(K^3)$ $O(KNT)$

Continued

Table 4.1 Summarized Consensus Functions—cont'd

Algorithm	Advantages	Disadvantages	Computing Complexity
SCECMGA (Analoui and Sadighian, 2007)	• Good ability to handle missing data in the case of missing cluster labels for certain patterns in the ensembles • Operates with arbitrary partitions with varying numbers of clusters • Uses the genetic algorithm to produce the most stable partitions • Uses a correlation matrix to find the best samples • Excellent scalability of the proposed genetic algorithm • Comprehensible model for clustering of large data sets • Selects clusters with the least perturbation from multiple partitions by objective function	• High computational cost • Unsuitable accuracy	$O(N^2)$

Although these consensus functions summarized in Table 4.1 have implemented in different ways and behaves differently based on their advantages, disadvantages, and computational complexity, there is a taxonomy appearing in the study by Ghaemi et al. (2009) to further classify these consensus functions based on the similar principle, which results five categories of consensus functions in clustering ensemble including hypergraphic partitioning approach, the coassociation-based approach, the voting-based approach, mutual information–based approach, and finite mixture model. Based on the simplicity in implementation, computational complexity, and clustering performance, three of these approaches specially draw our attention and provide the fundamental concepts to propose three clustering ensemble models presented in this book.

In the proposed *Hidden Markov Model (HMM)-based meta clustering ensemble* presented in Chapter 5, hypergraphic partitioning-based consensus functions are employed to combine the multiple clustering results by transforming the original problem domain to the hypergraphic-based domain, which easily avoids the corresponding problem inherited in most of the clustering ensemble algorithms and is quite flexible to apply any graphic-based clustering algorithm on the hypergraphic-based domain to produce a quality and robust ensemble solution. However, these approaches are often time consuming and intractable implementation for a large data set, especially time series data sets, which is demonstrated in our simulation described in Section 5.3.

Thus, we introduce the voting-based consensus function into another proposed clustering ensemble model, *Iteratively constructed clustering ensemble with a hybrid sampling*, presented in Chapter 6. In this approach, the implementation of voting-based consensus becomes much simpler, and significantly reduces the computational cost, which is demonstrated in the simulation described in Section 6.3, than the hypergraphic partitioning-based consensus functions. However, this approach has to explicitly solve the corresponding problem in order to produce a meaningful combination of multiple clustering results. Moreover, it requires that the input partitions must have the same number of clusters, which potentially cause infeasibility in the real-world applications.

Derived from above clustering ensemble models, our proposed clustering ensemble model *Weighted clustering ensemble with multiple representations* presented in Chapter 7 uses the coassociation-based consensus function to provide a trade-off ensemble solution between computational cost and clustering performance. By modifying the existing coassociation-based consensus function, our proposed coassociation-based consensus function named dendrogram-based similarity partitioning algorithm (DSPA) not only results a comparably high robustness in the ensemble solution but also has an ability to automatically determine the number of clusters in the final partition, which is demonstrated on various time series data sets in Section 7.3.

4.5.1.1 Hypergraphic Partitioning Approach

In hypergraphic partitioning, the clusters can be represented as hyperedges on a graph with vertices corresponding to the objects for clustering. Thus, each hyperedge describes a set of objects belonging to the same clusters. This reduces the problem of consensus clustering to simply finding the minimum cut of a hypergraph.

In the work proposed by Strehl and Ghosh (2003), multiple partitions are first mapped onto a hypergraph where its edge, named the hyperdge, is allowed to connect any set of vertices. In the hypergraph, one vertex corresponds to one object in the data set and one cluster forms an edge linked to all objects in the cluster. For example, there are three clustering results based on the same input data. Table 4.2 shows their label vectors and Table 4.3 shows the corresponding hypergraph.

In the hypergraph representation, a data set of N objects $\{x_n\}_{n=1}^{N}$ is represented as the vertices of the hypergraph. The hyperedge, h_i, is a generalization of an edge in that it can connect any set of vertices, which is a column of the matrix for the corresponding cluster, and the entry of a column with 1 indicates that relative objects are grouped into the corresponding cluster and 0 otherwise. Thus, concatenating

Table 4.2 Example of Clustering Ensemble (Label V)

	P_1	P_2	P_3
X_1	1	2	3
X_2	1	2	3
X_3	1	2	2
X_4	2	3	2
X_5	2	3	1
X_6	3	1	1
X_7	3	1	1

Table 4.3 Exmaple of Clustering Ensemble (Hypergraphic)

	H^1	H^2	H^3
	$h_1\ h_2\ h_3$	$h_4\ h_5\ h_6$	$h_7\ h_8\ h_9$
V_1	1 0 0	0 1 0	1 0 0
V_2	1 0 0	0 1 0	1 0 0
V_3	1 0 0	0 1 0	0 1 0
V_4	0 1 0	0 0 1	0 1 0
V_5	0 1 0	0 0 1	0 0 1
V_6	0 0 1	1 0 0	0 0 1
V_7	0 0 1	1 0 0	0 0 1

all hyperedge of multiple partitions leads to an adjacency matrix $H = \{h_i\}\sum_{i=1}^{k_t}$, where k_t is the number of clusters in the partition t, by all objects in the data set versus all the available clusters. In this example, the number of vertices (number of objects) is 7, and the number of hyperedges $(k_1 + k_2 + k_3)$ is 9.

Cluster-Based Similarity Partitioning Algorithm

For each input partition, an $N \times N$ binary similarity matrix encodes the piecewise similarity between any two objects, that is, the similarity of one indicates that two objects are grouped into the same cluster and a similarity of zero otherwise. The coassociation matrix S, which is an entrywise average of all $N \times N$ binary similarity matrices, can be calculated by adjacency matrix H: $S = HH^T$ via multiple-round clustering analyses. It is assumed that a pair of input patterns in the "natural" cluster is more likely to be colocated in the same clusters in different clustering. Therefore, we can construct the cluster-based similarity partitioning algorithm (CSPA) by the following steps:

1. Use multiple clustering results to establish a coassociation matrix based on the measure of pairwise similarity

2. Partition the hypergraph obtained from the coassociation matrix to produce a single clustering by a graphic-based clustering algorithm such as METIS (Karypis and Kumar, 1999).

The clustering ensemble model based on such consensus function can also be described by a pseudo code:

Input:

- *a set of input partitions {P_1, P_2,..., P_T}, with number of partitions T*
- *The graphic-based clustering algorithm METIS*

for t = 1 to T
      Find the number of clusters k_t in partition P_t
      for i = 1 to k_t
            construct the hyper-edge h_i
      end for
end for
Compute the adjacency matrix $H = \{h_i\} \sum_{i=1} k_t$

Compute the co-association matrix $\mathbf{S} = HH^T$
$K = \max(k_t)$
$P_{consensus} = METIS(S, K)$
Output: the final clustering $P_{consensus}$.

Fig. 4.1 shows the CSPA for the clustering ensemble example problem given in Table 4.2. Each entry of the similarity matrix has a value between 0 and 1 (gray level), which is proportional to how likely a pair of input patterns is in the same cluster.

Hypergraph-Partitioning Algorithm

This hypergraph-partitioning algorithm (HGPA) (Strehl and Ghosh, 2003) offers a consensus function by casting the clustering ensemble problem into how to partition the hypergraph by cutting a minimal number of hyperedges. Such a graph partitioning problem has been well studied in graph theory, and the hypergraph partitioning package, HMETIS (Karypis et al., 1997) has been used in this work (Strehl and Ghosh, 2003). Unlike the CSPA that takes the local piecewise similarity into account, the HGPA considers a relatively global relationship of objects across different partitions. In addition, the function has one property that tends to yield a final

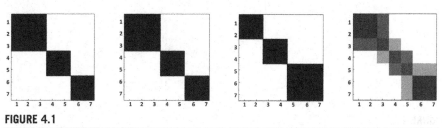

FIGURE 4.1

CSPA similarity matrix.

partition where all clusters are of approximately the same size. Therefore, the HGPA can be constructed by following steps:

1. Construct a hypergraph obtained from input partitions, where each hyperedge describes a set of objects belonging to the same clusters with equal weights, in form of adjacency matrix H.
2. Use hypergraph partitioning package, HMETIS (Karypis et al., 1997) to segment the hypergraph to produce a single consensus clustering by cutting a minimal number of hyperedges

A pseudo code is also given to describe this consensus function:
Input:

- *a set of input partitions $\{P_1, P_2, ..., P_T\}$, with number of partitions T*
- *The graphic-based clustering algorithm HMETIS*

> *for $t = 1$ to T*
> > *Find the number of clusters k_t in partition P_t*
> > *for $i = 1$ to k_t*
> > > *construct the hyper-edge h_i*
> > *end for*
> *end for*
> *Compute the adjacency matrix*

$$H = \{h_i\} \sum_{i=1} k_t$$
$$K = \max(k_t)$$
$$P_{consensus} = HMETIS(H, K)$$
Output: the final clustering $P_{consensus}$.

For the same clustering ensemble example problem in Table 4.2, Fig. 4.2 shows that each hyperedge is represented by a closed curve enclosing the vertices it connects. The combined clustering $\{(x1,x2,x3), (x4,x5), (x6,x7)\}$ cuts these hyperedges with a minimal number of 2 and is balanced as possible for three clusters of seven objects.

Meta-Clustering Algorithm

The meta-clustering algorithm (MCLA) (Strehl and Ghosh, 2003) is based on obtained clusters. Each cluster is represented by a hyperedge in the hypergraph.

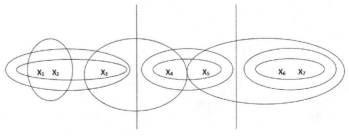

FIGURE 4.2

HGPA hyperedge cutting.

We group the related hyperedges as a meta-cluster C^m and collapse the related hyperedges by assigning each input item to the collapsed hyperedge in which it participates most strongly. We then reduce the number of hyperedges from $\sum k_t$ to K. The entire process of MCLA is comprised of four steps:

1. Construct meta-graph: the hyperedges h_i, $\forall t$ of the hypergraph are represented as vertices in the meta-graph. The edge weights are proportional to the similarity between vertices. The binary Jaccard measure is used as the similarity measure, which is the ratio of the intersection to the union of the sets of input patterns corresponding to the two hyperedges shown as: $w_{a,b} = \dfrac{h_a^T h_b}{\|h_a\|_2^2 + \|h_b\|_2^2 - h_a^T h_b}$, where h_a and h_b are two hyperedges representing two vertices in the meta-graph, and $w_{a,b}$ is the edge weight between two vertices.

2. Cluster hyperedges: matching labels are found by partitioning the meta-graph into k balanced meta-clusters. Each vertex is weighted proportionally to the size of the corresponding cluster. Balancing ensures that the sum of vertex weights is approximately the same in each meta-cluster. Graph partitioning package METIS is used in this step resulting in a clustering of the h vectors. As each vertex in the meta-graph represents a distinct cluster label, a meta-cluster represents a group of corresponding labels.

3. Collapse meta-clusters: the related hyperedges of a meta-cluster are collapsed into a single meta-hyperedge in the meta-graph. For each meta-cluster, an association vector h_k^m is calculated by an entrywise average of the corresponding h vectors, which indicates how strongly the corresponding input pattern associates with this meta-cluster.

4. Compete for objects: according to the association vectors, the input pattern has to be assigned to the meta-cluster with the highest entry. The input pattern is assigned to the meta-cluster with the highest entry in the association vector. Ties are broken randomly. The confidence of an assignment is reflected by the winner's share of association (ratio of the winner's association to the sum of all other associations). Note that not every meta-cluster can be guaranteed to win at least one object. Thus, there are at most K labels in the final combined clustering.

The clustering ensemble model based on such consensus function can be also described by a pseudo code:

Input:

- *a set of input partitions $\{P_1, P_2, ..., P_T\}$, with number of partitions T*
- *The graphic-based clustering algorithm METIS*

> *for $t = 1$ to T*
> > *Find the number of clusters k_t in partition P_t*
> > *for $i = 1$ to k_t*
> > > *construct the hyper-edge h_i*
> > *end for*

end for

Compute the adjacency matrix $H = \{h_i\} \sum\limits_{i=1} k_t$

for $a = 1$ to Σk_i

   for $b = 1$ to Σk_i

      Compute the edge weights of meta-graph $w_{a,b} = \dfrac{h_a^T h_b}{\|h_a\|_2^2 + \|h_b\|_2^2 - h_a^T h_b}$

   end for

end for

Construct a matrix of edge weights $W = \left[w_{a,b}\right]_{a=1,2,\ldots,\Sigma k_i}^{b=1,2,\ldots,\Sigma k_i}$

$K = \max(k_t)$

$P^m = METIS(W, H, K)$

for $k = 1$ to K

   compute association vector $h_k^m = \dfrac{1}{\|C_K^m\|} \sum\limits_{C_i \in C_K^m} h_i$ for meta cluster C_k^m in

   partition P^m of meta-graph

end for

$P_{consensus}(x) = \arg \max\limits_{k=1,\ldots K} h_k^m(x)$

Output: the final clustering $P_{consensus}$.

For the given clustering ensemble example in Tables 4.2 and 4.3, we consider the first meta-cluster C_1^m associated with corresponding vectors $\{h_3, h_4, h_9\}$ and collapse the hyperedges of the meta-cluster by calculating the association vector $h_1^m = (0, 0, 0, 0, 1/3, 1, 1)$ and apply the same procedure for the rest of meta-clusters. Hence, the C_1^m wins the input pattern X6 and X7. $C_1^m = (x_6, x_7)$, subsequently results in the label of the final clustering result (2,2,2,3,3,1,1).

4.5.1.2 Coassociation-Based Approach

In this approach, a coassociation matrix is initially generated by the measure of pairwise similarity based on multiple input partitions, and numerous hierarchical agglomerative algorithms can be applied to the coassociation matrix to obtain the consensus partition.

In hypergraphic partitioning-based consensus functions lie major drawbacks of the cluster number in final clustering has to be manually predefined, or is equal to the largest cluster number among multiple clustering. A coassociation-based consensus function is therefore proposed. This is a DSPA (Yang, 2006) that is able to automatically determine the number of clusters in the final partitioning. The entire process of DSPA consists of following steps:

1. Construct a coassociation matrix used to reflect the relationship among all items in multiple partitions, where the element at location (i, j) describes the similarity defined as the number of occurrences as two objects i and j are grouped into the same cluster

2. Converts the coassociation matrix into a dendrogram, where the horizontal axis indexes the objectives in the given data sets and the vertical axis indicates the lifetimes of clusters. The lifetime of clusters in the dendrogram is defined as an interval from the time the cluster is established to the time the cluster disappears by merging with other clusters.

3. Apply a hierarchical clustering algorithm on the dendrogram to produce the consensus partition and automatically determine the number of clusters in a consensus partition by cutting the dendrogram at a range of threshold values corresponding to the longest cluster's lifetime.

The clustering ensemble model based on such consensus function can be described by a pseudo code:

Input:

- *a set of input partitions $\{P_1, P_2,..., P_T\}$, with number of partitions T*
- *the hierarchical clustering algorithm HCLUSTER*

    for t = 1 to T
        Find the number of clusters k_t in partition
        for i = 1 to k_t
            construct the hyper-edge h_i
        end for
    end for
    Compute the adjacency matrix $H = \{h_i\} \sum_{i=1} k_t$
    Compute the co-association matrix $S = HH^T$
    Construct the a dendrogram G based on the co-association matrix S
    Define a threshold Θ based on the longest cluster's lifetime in the dendrogram G
    $P_{consensus} = HCLUSTER(G, \Theta)$
    Output: the final clustering $P_{consensus}$.

For the given cluster ensemble example in Table 4.2, Fig. 4.3 shows the dendrogram based on the corresponding coassociation matrix. The cluster lifetimes are identified with 2 clusters: $L2 = 0.1$, 3 clusters: $L3 = 0.5$, 5 clusters: $L5 = 0.3$. Final partitioning, based on the 3 clusters corresponding to the longest lifetime, is chosen.

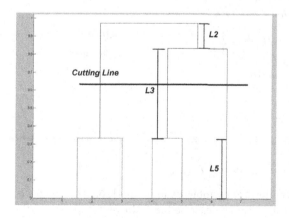

FIGURE 4.3

DSPA cutting line.

4.5.1.3 Voting-Based Approach

The voting approach attempts to solve the correspondence problem. Then, a simple voting schema such as majority voting can be used to assign objects in clusters to determine the final consensus partition. However, label correspondence is exactly what makes unsupervised combination difficult. The main idea is to permute the cluster labels so that best agreement between the labels of two partitions is obtained. All the partitions from the ensemble must be relabeled according to a fixed reference partition. The reference partition can be taken from the ensemble or from a new partition of the data set.

In this approach, the cluster number in each input partition has to be the same as in the reference partition, entire procedure simply involves two steps:

1. Use Hungarian algorithm (Winston and Goldberg, 1994) to reassign the labels of input partitions with selected reference partition such as one of ensemble members.
2. Apply the majority voting onto the relabeled input partitions to produce the cluster label of final consensus partition

This consensus function can be also described by a pseudo code:
Input:

- *an integer K (cluster number results in all input partitions)*
- *an integer N (number of objects/size of dataset)*
- *a set of input partitions {P_1, P_2,..., P_T}, with number of partitions T*
- *a reference partition $P' = P_1$*
- *the Hungarian algorithm HUNGARIAN*

> *for t = 1 to T*
> > *re-assign the label of input partition: $P'_t = HUNGARIAN(P', P_t)$*
>
> *end for*
> $P' = \{P'_t\}_t^T$
> *for t = 1 to T*
> > *for n = 1 to N*
> > > *for k = 1 to K*
> > > $$H_t^{n,k} = \begin{cases} 1 & \text{if data n is assigned to cluster j in } P'_t \\ 0 & \text{Otherwise} \end{cases}$$
> > > *end for*
> > *end for*
> *end for*
> *for n = 1 to N*
> > $P_{consensus}(x_n) = \arg\max_k \sum_t^T w_t H_t^{n,k} \text{ where } w_t = 1/T, \forall t,$
> *end for*
> *Output: the final clustering $P_{consensus}$.*

For the given cluster ensemble example in Table 4.3 again, the application of Hungarian algorithm can be described in following steps:

1. Determine a reference partition $P' = P_1$, (1,1,1,2,2,3,3), and construct a pairwise dissimilarity matrix between clusters obtained by reference partition P' and

matching matrix P_3 (3,3,2,2,1,1,1) separately. This matrix is calculated by $DisM_{i,j}(P',P_t) = Z - |C_i \cap C_j|$ where $Z = 3$, is maximum size of cluster in both of partitions.

	C_1^3	C_2^3	C_3^3
C_1'	3	2	1
C_2'	2	2	3
C_3'	1	3	3

2. Subtract the smallest number in each row from every number in the row. This is called a row reduction. Enter the results in a new table.

	C_1^3	C_2^3	C_3^3
C_1'	2	1	0
C_2'	0	0	1
C_3'	0	2	2

3. Subtract the smallest number in each column of the new table from every number in the column. This is called a column reduction. Enter the results in another table.

	C_1^3	C_2^3	C_3^3
C_1'	2	1	0
C_2'	0	0	1
C_3'	0	2	2

4. Test whether an optimum assignment can be made by determining the minimum number of lines needed to cover (i.e., cross out) all zeros. If the number of lines equals the number of rows, an optimum assignment is possible. In this case, go to Step 7. Otherwise go on to Step 5.

	$C_1^{\,3}$	$C_2^{\,3}$	$C_3^{\,3}$
C_1'	2	1	0
C_2'	0	0	1
C_3'	0	2	2

5. If the number of lines is less than the number of rows, modify the table in this way:
   a. Subtract the smallest uncovered number from every uncovered number in the table.

    b. Add the smallest uncovered number to the numbers at intersections of covering lines.

    c. Numbers crossed out but not at intersections of crossout lines carry over unchanged to the next table.

6. Repeat Steps 3 and 4 until an optimal table is obtained.

7. Make the assignments. Begin with rows or columns with only one zero. Match items that have zeros, using only one match for each row and each column. Cross out both the rows and the columns after the match. $C_1' - C_3^3, C_2' - C_2^3, C_3' - C_1^3$.

After an overall consistent relabeling, the reassigned label results, based on the three input partitions, are shown in Table 4.4. Then majority voting can be simply applied to determine cluster membership for each object, where the label of consensus partition is assigned by the majority of input partitions. The label of consensus partition is (1,1,1,2,2,3,3).

4.5.2 OBJECTIVE FUNCTION

Although the individual use of various consensus functions can yield a single consensus partition, performance differs when applied to data sets of various characteristics. Without prior information, selecting a proper consensus function in advance to form a clustering ensemble is impossible. As with the cluster ensemble proposed in the early work of Strehl and Ghosh (2003), a normalized mutual-information–based objective function (Strehl and Ghosh, 2003) is proposed for measuring the consistency between any two partitions:

$$\text{NMI}(P_a, P_b) = \frac{\sum_{i=1}^{K_a} \sum_{j=1}^{K_b} N_{ij}^{ab} \log\left(\frac{N N_{ij}^{ab}}{N_i^a N_j^b}\right)}{\sqrt{\left(\sum_{i=1}^{K_a} N_i^a \log\left(\frac{N_i^a}{N}\right)\right)\left(\sum_{j=1}^{K_b} N_j^b \log\left(\frac{N_j^b}{N}\right)\right)}}. \quad (4.4)$$

Here, P_a and P_b are labeling for two partitions that divide a data set of N objects into K_a and K_b clusters, respectively. N_i^a denotes the number of objects in cluster $C_i^a \in P_a$ and N_j^b the number of objects in cluster $C_j^b \in P_b$. N_{ij}^{ab} is the number of shared objects

Table 4.4 Reassigned Label

	P_1	P_2	P_3
X_1	1	1	1
X_2	1	1	1
X_3	1	1	2
X_4	2	2	2
X_5	2	2	3
X_6	3	3	3
X_7	3	3	3

between clusters C_i^a and C_j^b. Therefore, the mutual information $I(P_a, P_b)$ between P_a and P_b labeling variables is calculated by $\sum_{i=1}^{K_a} \sum_{j=1}^{K_b} N_{ij}^{ab} \log\left(\frac{NN_{ij}^{ab}}{N_i^a N_j^b}\right)$. However, the mutual information does not have an upper bound. For easy interpretation and comparisons, a normalized version of mutual information $\text{NMI}(P_a, P_b)$ is formulated as $\frac{I(P_a, P_b)}{\sqrt{H(P_a)H(P_b)}}$, where $H(P_a)$ denotes the entropy of P_a labeling variable calculated by $\sum_{i=1}^{K_a} N_i^a \log\left(\frac{N_i^a}{N}\right)$ and $H(P_b)$ denotes the entropy of P_b calculated by $\sum_{j=1}^{K_b} N_j^b \log\left(\frac{N_j^b}{N}\right)$. Based on (4.4), the optimal final partition can be determined by finding out the one that possesses maximal average mutual information with all T partitions available from multiple-round clustering analyses prior to the clustering ensemble (Strehl and Ghosh, 2003). Thus, finding the proper one from R various consensus functions can be performed by

$$P^* = \text{argmax}_{1 \le r \le R} \sum_{t=1}^{T} \text{NMI}(P_r, P_t). \tag{4.5}$$

In other words, the consensus function yielding the partition P^* is the correct one for the given data set.

4.6 SUMMARY

For ensemble learning, we have given the definition of ensemble in a manner of supervised learning and addressed the fundamental problems of ensemble learning: how to train each of base learners (ensemble learning algorithms), how to combine the outputs obtained from the multiple base learner (combining methods), and what is the critical factor to determine the success of ensemble learning (ensemble diversity). In ensemble learning algorithms, we have described both bagging and boosting algorithms which gave the initial inspiration to propose the *Iteratively constructed clustering ensemble model* presented in Chapter 6. In combining methods, linear, product, and majority voting combiners have been described in detail. Moreover, we have discussed the diversity issue related to the success of ensemble learning.

For the clustering ensemble, we have studied the problem of combining multiple partitions known as consensus function. By using a simple example, various consensus functions used in our proposed ensemble models described in the latter chapters are detailed in terms of a hypergraphic-based, a coassociation-based, and a voting-based approach. We have identified that three consensus functions based on a hypergraphic-partition approach (Strehl and Ghosh, 2003) suffer from a major weakness, that is, the number of clusters in a final partition needs to be determined manually in advance or we must simply use the maximal number of clusters appearing in multiple partitions for model selection. Motivated by the clustering ensemble based on evidence accumulation (Fred and Jain, 2005), we therefore introduce an alternative consensus function—DSPA—based on a coassociation approach that can automatically determine the number of clusters in the final partition by cutting the dendrogram at a range of threshold values corresponding to the longest cluster's lifetime. Eventually, we present a simple consensus function based on majority voting, which is used in our proposed *Iterative constructed clustering ensemble model* to be described in Chapter 6.

HMM-Based Hybrid Meta-Clustering in Association With Ensemble Technique

5

5.1 INTRODUCTION

For model-based clustering approaches, we consider that each time series is generated by some kind of model or by a mixture of underlying probability distributions. Temporal data are considered similar when the models characterizing individual data or the remaining residuals after fitting the model are similar, based on the likelihood distance measures. The model type is often specified a priori, such as the Gaussian (Banfield and Raftery, 1993) or Hidden Markov models (Panuccio et al., 2009). The model structure (e.g., the number of hidden states in a Hidden Markov Model [HMM]) can be determined by model-selection techniques. While model parameters can be estimated by using maximum likelihood algorithms, for example, the expectation-maximization (EM) algorithm (Bilmes, 1998). The entire process of such approaches therefore aims to estimate the optimal parameters of components models with maximum log-likelihood.

HMM, an important model-based approach for temporal data clustering, has been studied for the last decade. Although HMM has outstanding ability in capturing temporal features whose values change significantly during the observation period, thereby satisfying the Markov property, it still suffers from the critical model-selection problems of finding the appropriate HMM model configuration and selecting the intrinsic number of clusters.

Temporal Data Mining via Unsupervised Ensemble Learning. http://dx.doi.org/10.1016/B978-0-12-811654-8.00005-1

In this chapter, we therefore present HMM-based hybrid meta-clustering in association with ensemble technique for temporal data. In this approach, clustering ensemble technique is used to tackle both the model-selection and initialization problems, and the hybrid meta-clustering aims to, at once, improve clustering results and reduce computational cost. The proposed approach yields favorable results, having been demonstrated on a set of data sets.

The rest of chapter will be presented as follows. First, we state the motivation of our proposed approach and follow it with model description. Then, the experimental results based on the various data sets including HMM-generated data set, synthetic time series (Cylinder-Bell-Funnel [CBF]), a collection of time series benchmarks, and motion trajectories database (CAVIAR) are reported in the simulation section. Finally, we conclude our proposed approach and discuss future work.

5.2 HMM-BASED HYBRID META-CLUSTERING ENSEMBLE

In this section, we briefly analyze HMM model-based clustering algorithms that are related to our proposed model. Based on their weaknesses and strengths, we then describe our motivation for proposing our model. Then, the model description is presented in detail.

5.2.1 MOTIVATION

Generally, standard model-based clustering algorithms can be classified within two major approaches; model-based partitioning and hierarchical clustering. For the standard HMM-clustering algorithms, the HMM-based K-models should be categorized into the model-based partitioning approach, and HMM-based agglomerative and divisive clustering should be categorized into the model-based hierarchical approach. According to early studies on these algorithms, we can deduce that each has a different weakness when applied to temporal data clustering. For instance, HMM-based K-models suffer from the model-selection and initialization problems inherent in conventional K-means algorithms. Although HMM-based agglomerative and divisive clustering can avoid the initialization problem, they still incur high computational costs in temporal data—clustering tasks. However, a model-based hybrid partitioning-hierarchical clustering and its variants (Zhong and Ghosh, 2003) have been proposed to combine the strengths of partitioning and hierarchical approaches.

As mentioned in Section 3.2.4, HMM-based hybrid partitional-hierarchical clustering (Zhong and Ghosh, 2003) is essentially an improved version of HMM-based agglomerative clustering, keeping some hierarchical structure. By associating with HMM-based K-models clustering, the complexity of input data for the agglomerative clustering is relatively reduced, requiring less computational cost. However, the initial flat-partitioned clusters are still produced by HMM-based K-models as a generative of K-means. Therefore, this hybrid clustering still suffers from the initialization problem existed in K-means algorithm and leaves the major model-selection problem (selecting an intrinsic number of clusters) unresolved. On the other hand, HMM-based hierarchical meta-clustering (Zhong and Ghosh, 2003) makes further improvements on the previous model, which provides two major benefits for temporal data clustering. Firstly, no re-estimation of merged models is required because the composite model can be represented by the parameters of its children. Therefore, computational complexity is significantly reduced. Second, a composite model more efficiently captures the character of the complex structure of cluster than a single model which is more difficult to define and train. However, the meta-data as inputs for agglomerative clustering are obtained by using HMM-based K-models, which still causes the initialization problem and still suffers from the model-selection problem.

Although both algorithms have a number of strength for temporal data—clustering tasks, they still crucially suffer from the initialization sensitivity and model-selection problem existed in most of common model-based approaches. Hence, motivated by our earlier studies on unsupervised ensemble learning (Yang and Chen, 2006, 2007) for temporal data—clustering problems, a novel model-based clustering approach is proposed by associating HMM-based hierarchical meta-clustering with ensemble technique, where initialization problem would be addressed by combining the multiple partitions obtained by HMM-based K-models into a single robust consensus partition as inputs of agglomerative clustering, and the appropriate cluster number can be automatically determined by applying proposed consensus function, Dendrogram-based Similarity Partitioning Algorithm (DSPA) (Yang and Chen, 2006) to the multiple partitions of target temporal data during the ensemble process. Moreover, this proposed algorithm still inherent excellence from original HHM-based hierarchical meta-clustering such as that composite model has an outstanding ability to characterize the complex-structured clusters, and no parameter re-estimation is required for the new merged pair of clusters, serving to reduce computational cost.

5.2.2 MODEL DESCRIPTION

The proposed approach is modified version of HMM-based hierarchical meta-clustering described in Section 3.2.4, which consists of three modules; that is, HMM-based K-models clustering, clustering ensemble, and HMM-based agglomerative clustering. In this approach, the ensemble learning technique is implemented to overcome the initialization problem caused by HMM-based K-models clustering during initial clustering analysis. By associating with proposed consensus function (DSPA), the intrinsic number of clusters would be automatically determined during the clustering ensemble phase. In addition to Fig. 5.1, an algorithm description is given below:

1. Produce a set of partitions by applying HMM-based K-models clustering on the target data under different initialization conditions and randomly select a K value from a preset range, $K^* - 2 \leq K \leq 2K^* + 1$ $(K > 0)$.
2. Combine the collection of multiple partitions obtained by HMM-based K-models clustering to form the consensus partitions based on three consensus functions (Cluster-based Similarity Partitioning Algorithm -CSPA, Hyper Graph-Partitioning Algorithm -HGPA, and Meta-CLustering Algorithm -MCLA) described in Section 4.5.1.1.

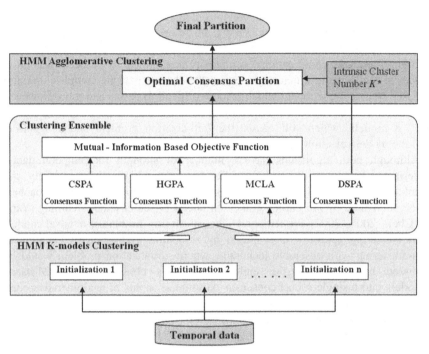

FIGURE 5.1

HMM-based hybrid meta-clustering associating with ensemble technique.

3. Apply DSPA consensus function detailed in Section 4.5.1.2 separately onto the collection of multiple partitions in order to determine the intrinsic number of clusters K'.

4. Select an optimal consensus partition $P_{optimal}$ from three candidates by using the mutual information–based objective function detailed in Section 4.5.2.

5. Re-estimate HMM model parameters for the optimal consensus partition $P_{optimal}$ by using EM algorithm.

6. Calculate the intercluster distances of optimal consensus partition by using a symmetric version of BoundaryKL distance measure

$$D^{boundary}(\lambda_i, \lambda_j) = \frac{1}{|x|} \sum_{x \in C_i \cup C_j} (\log p(x|\lambda_i) - \log p(x|\lambda_j)) \text{ where } (C_i, C_j) \in$$

$P_{optimal}$ represent cluster i and j in optimal consensus partition $P_{optimal}$, respectively. The closest pair of clusters is merged to form a composite model $\lambda_{i,j} = \{\lambda_i, \lambda_j\}$, and the distance between two composite models is defined as

$$D(\lambda_a, \lambda_b) = \frac{1}{|\lambda_a| \times |\lambda_b|} \sum_{\lambda'_a \in \lambda_a} \sum_{\lambda'_b \in \lambda_b} D^{boundary}(\lambda'_a, \lambda'_b). \text{ The process of merging clus-}$$

ters is repeated until the determined number of clusters K' reached.

A pseudocode is also given.

Input:

- *a data set $X = \{x_1, x_2, \ldots, x_N\}$.*
- *an integer K^* (intrinsic cluster number)*
- *an integer T (number of partitions)*
- *an integer M (number of HMM model states)*
- *the HMM-based K-models clustering HMMkm*
- *the expectation-maximization (EM) algorithm EM*
- *A NMI based objective function NMI*
- *Clustering ensemble ENSEMBLE*

> *for $t = 1$ to T*
>   *$K = RAND\{K^* - 2 \leq K \leq 2K^* + 1\}$*
>   *$P_t = HMMkm(K, M, X)$*
> *end for*
> *$P = \{P_1, P_2, \ldots P_T\}$*
> *$[P_{CSPA}, P_{HGPA}, P_{MCLA}] = ENSEMBLE(P)$*
> *$K' = DSPA(P)$*
> *$[P_{optimal}, K_{optimal}] = NMI(P_{CSPA}, P_{HGPA}, P_{MCLA})$*
> *$\lambda_{optimal} = EM(P_{optimal}, M)$*
> *$K_{agg} = K_{optimal}$*
> *while $K_{agg} > K'$*
>
> $$D(\lambda_a, \lambda_b) = \min_{(\lambda_a, \lambda_b) \in \lambda_{optimal}} \frac{1}{|\lambda_a| \times |\lambda_b|} \sum_{\lambda'_a \in \lambda_a} \sum_{\lambda'_b \in \lambda_b} D^{boundary}\left(\lambda'_a, \lambda'_b\right) \text{ where}$$
>
> $$D^{boundary}(\lambda_i, \lambda_j) = \frac{1}{|x|} \sum_{x \in C_i \cup C_j} (\log p(x|\lambda_i) - \log p(x|\lambda_j)) \text{ and } (C_i, C_j) \in P_{optimal}$$
>
> Update clustering structure
> $\lambda_{a,b} = \{\lambda_a, \lambda_a\}; \quad C_{a,b} = \{C_a, C_a\};$
> $\lambda_{optimal} = \lambda_{optimal} / \{\lambda_a, \lambda_a\} \cap \lambda_{a,b}$
> $P_{optimal} = P_{optimal} / \{C_a, C_a\} \cap C_{a,b}$
> $K_{agg} = K_{agg} - 1;$
> end while
> $P_{agg} = P_{optimal}$
> *Output*:
> the final clustering P_{agg}

5.3 SIMULATION

In this section, we evaluate the performance of our proposed clustering ensemble model for solving initialization and model-selection problems. The proposed ensemble model results are reported and compared with similar methods on HMM-generated data set, synthetic time series named CBF, time series benchmark, and CAVIAR database of motion trajectories.

5.3.1 HMM-GENERATED DATA SET

In the first phase of experiments, we evaluate the performance of our approach in comparison to various relative algorithms. Standard HMM-clustering algorithms including K-models, agglomerative and divisive clustering, HMM-based hybrid clustering, and HMM-based hybrid meta-clustering (detailed in Section 3.2.4), are concurrently applied on the HMM-generated data set.

Taking a similar approach to the work (Smyth, 1997), a total of 200 HMM-generated data are produced from a mixture of four HMM components, and each continuous HMM model generates 50 sequences with an identical length of 200. The generation function is stated as,

$$p(X|\lambda) = 0.25p(X|\lambda_1) + 0.25p(X|\lambda_2) + 0.25p(X|\lambda_3) + 0.25p(X|\lambda_4) \qquad (5.1)$$

$$\lambda_k = \left(\pi_k, A_k, \mu_k, \sigma_k^2\right) \qquad (5.2)$$

where each HMM model has two hidden states with transition parameters $A_1 = \begin{bmatrix} 0.6 & 0.4 \\ 0.4 & 0.6 \end{bmatrix}$, $A_2 = \begin{bmatrix} 0.4 & 0.6 \\ 0.6 & 0.4 \end{bmatrix}$, $A_3 = \begin{bmatrix} 0.3 & 0.7 \\ 0.7 & 0.3 \end{bmatrix}$, $A_4 = \begin{bmatrix} 0.7 & 0.3 \\ 0.3 & 0.7 \end{bmatrix}$, the emission distribution corresponding to each state is distributed as a single Gaussian, mean $\mu_k^1 = 3$, variance $\sigma_k^{1^2} = 1$ for state 1, and mean $\mu_k^2 = 0$, variance $\sigma_k^{2^2} = 1$ for state 2. The initial state probabilities π_k are randomly generated by uniform distribution.

The clustering performance depends heavily on the selection of input parameter K. However, this important input parameter K cannot be automatically determined by the most of algorithms themselves and needs to be selected manually. In contrast, our proposed clustering ensemble model runs the HMM-K-models for initial clustering analysis with number of states—four and a randomly selected K value as cluster number from a preset range $K^* - 1 \leq K \leq K^* + 2$ ($K > 0$) instead of manually selected number of clusters, which produces 10 partitions on the target data set. These input partitions are used to construct the final partition, and the cluster number of final partition is automatically determined by DSPA consensus function. Fig. 5.2 represents the dendrogram produced by applying DSPA consensus function on 10 input partitions, where correct number of clusters represented by four different colored subtree is automatically detected by cutting the dendrogram at a range of threshold values corresponding to the longest cluster's lifetime.

In comparison with the standard model-selection approach, we also apply our approach on the target data set by trying the fixed cluster size in a range of $2 \leq K \leq 10$ on restart and using the Bayesian information criterion (BIC). As illustrated in Fig. 5.3, the optimal number of clusters is selected as seven with a minimum value of BIC, which failed to determine the correct number of clusters ($K^* = 4$).

By prespecifying the number of states $M = 2$ and cluster number $K^* = 4$, clustering algorithms including HMM-K-models, HMM-agglomerative, HMM-divisive clustering, HMM-based hybrid clustering, and HMM-based hybrid meta-clustering are also applied to the target synthetic data with different model initializations. In contrast, our proposed clustering ensemble model runs the HMM K-models for initial

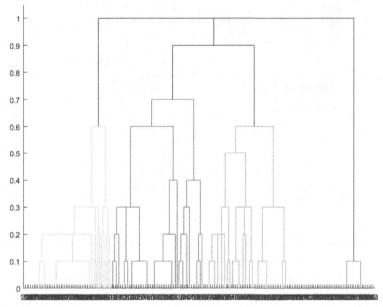

FIGURE 5.2

Dendrogram (HMM-generated data set).

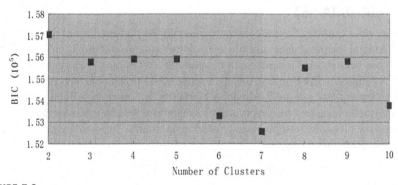

FIGURE 5.3

BIC on different number of clusters (HMM-generated data set).

clustering analysis with a randomly selected K value as cluster number from a preset range $K^* - 1 \leq K \leq K^* + 2$ $(K > 0)$ under different initialization conditions which produces 10 partitions on the target data set to produce the final partition. Each clustering algorithm is run 10 times. Average classification accuracy is presented in the form of mean $\pm$ standard deviation and illustrated in Table 5.1.

The top part of the Table shows the results for algorithms without model-selection ability from where the higher valued standard deviation in the

Table 5.1 Classification Accuracy (%) of Our HMM-Based Hybrid Meta-Clustering Ensemble on HMM-Generated Data Set

Clustering Algorithms	Average Classification Accuracy (Mean ± Std)
HMM K-model	73.2 ± 5.5
HMM agglomerative	71.1 ± 2.1
HMM divisive	68.5 ± 3.9
HMM hybrid clustering	73.8 ± 3.9
HMM hybrid meta-clustering	74.2 ± 2.6
Our approach	**83.1 ± 1.8**

Bold denotes best result

classification rate indicates that the performances of these clustering algorithms are unstabilized due to the model initialization problem. In contrast, the last row of Table 5.1 shows the averaged classification accuracy of proposed clustering ensemble model on the HMM-generated data with the higher averaged classification accuracy and smaller standard deviation, which indicates that our proposed ensemble model with model-selection ability is insensitive to the initialization.

5.3.2 CBF DATA SET

In the second experiment, we are going to evaluate the performance of our approach for the general temporal data—clustering tasks by using a synthetic time series. This data set has been used as a benchmark in temporal data mining (Keogh and Kasetty, 2003). As illustrated in Fig. 5.4, this data set is a 1-D time series named CBF consisting of three classes of data, cylinder (c), bell (b), or funnel (f). Although this data set is originally designed for supervised classification, we can use it for the purpose of testing the proposed unsupervised clustering approach. The data are generated by three time series functions:

$$c(t) = (6+k)x_{[a,b]}(t) + \varepsilon(t), \tag{5.3}$$

$$b(t) = (6+k)x_{[a,b]}(t)(t-a)/(b-a) + \varepsilon(t), \tag{5.4}$$

$$f(t) = (6+k)x_{[a,b]}(t)(t-b)/(b-a) + \varepsilon(t). \tag{5.5}$$

where k and $\varepsilon(t)$ are drawn from the normal distribution $N(0,1)$, a and b are two integers randomly drawn from intervals [16, 32] and [48, 128], and $x_{[a,b]}(t)$ is defined as 1 if $b \leq t \leq a$ and 0 otherwise. Three stochastic functions in (5.3-5.5) randomly generate a time series of 128 frames corresponding to three classes: cylinder, bell, and funnel. In our simulations, we generate 100 samples for each class and the whole data set contains 300 samples in total.

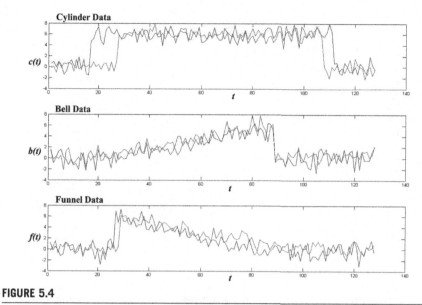

FIGURE 5.4

Cylinder-bell-funnel data set.

Following the same experiment setup in the first part of simulation, the performance of model selection based on the DSPA consensus function is compared with standard model-selection approach by applying our approach on the CBF data set with all cluster size ($2 \leq K \leq 10$) and using BIC model-selection criteria to detect the optimal number of clusters. In order to achieve the best parameter setup based on the target data set, the stated number of HMM models is set to seven by an exhaustive search. As illustrated in Fig. 5.5, the DSPA consensus automatically detects the correct number of clusters ($K^* = 3$) again represented in three different colored subtree. However, the wrong number of clusters ($K = 4$) is obtained by standard model-selection approach with a minimum value of BIC shown in Fig. 5.6. As a result, we trust that our approach based on Dendrogram-based Similarity Partitioning Algorithm (DSPA) consensus function has a better performance of model selection than the standard approach.

In order to compare the performance between our approach and relative HMM-based clustering algorithms, five clustering algorithms evaluated in the first part of the simulation are also applied to the CBF data set with the optimal number of states $M = 7$ and cluster number $K^* = 3$. For the proposed approach associated with ensemble technique, HMM k-models clustering initially produces various partitions of CBF data with different initialization and random selection of cluster numbers from a range $K^* - 1 \leq K \leq K^* + 2$ ($K > 0$). Then, three consensus functions (CSPA, HGPA, and MCLA) are applied to yield respective consensus partitions. Subsequently, the mutual information–based objective function determines the optimal consensus partition. The fourth consensus function DSPA is used to

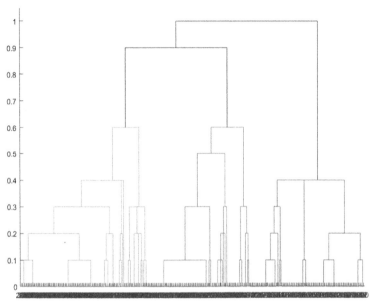

FIGURE 5.5

Dendrogram (Cylinder-bell-funnel data set).

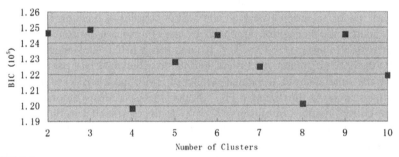

FIGURE 5.6

BIC on different number of clusters (Cylinder-bell-funnel data set).

automatically select the cluster number K^*. Finally, both the optimal consensus partitions obtained from the ensemble of HMM k-models clustering and the selected cluster number K^* are used as the input of HMM-agglomerative clustering to produce the final partition for the CBF data. We run each of clustering algorithms 10 times on the CBF data to obtain its average classification accuracy. As shown in Table 5.2, our approach once again yields a favorable result on the CBF data set when compared to the relative clustering algorithms, even given the best parameter setup (optimal number of states and correct number of clusters), which once again demonstrates the efficiency of our approach to solve model-selection and initialization problems for general temporal data—clustering tasks.

Table 5.2 Classification Accuracy (%) of Our HMM-Based Hybrid Meta-Clustering Ensemble on CBF Data Set

Clustering Algorithms	Average Classification Accuracy (Mean ± Std)
HMM K-model	65.2 ± 4.3
HMM agglomerative	71.1 ± 3.1
HMM divisive	64.5 ± 3.1
HMM- based hybrid clustering	69.8 ± 2.9
HMM hybrid meta-clustering	70.2 ± 2.5
Our approach	**77.9 ± 1.5**

Bold denotes best result

5.3.3 TIME SERIES BENCHMARKS

The previous experiment examines the legitimacy of the fundamental concept under certain assumptions, where the data sets are either HMM-generated data set or simple synthetic time series. In order to evaluate the performance of our approach for more general temporal data—clustering tasks, we implement another experiment by using a collection of several time series data set.

Time series benchmarks of 16 synthetic or real-world time series data sets (Keogh, 2003) have been collected to evaluate a number of classification and clustering algorithms in the context of temporal data mining. In this collection, the ground truth, that is, the class label of time series in a data set, is available, and each data set is further divided into the training and testing subsets in advance for the evaluation of a classification algorithm. The information on all 16 data sets is tabulated in Table 5.3, including the number of classes, the number of time series, and the length of time series in every data set. Although the outcome of clustering analysis can be used for miscellaneous tasks, we focus on only clustering-based classification tasks in simulations. By given the ground truth, the classification rate is defined as the ratio of the number of time series of the same class label that are grouped together into the same cluster to the overall number of time series of the data set.

In this experiment, we employ K-means, dynamic time warping (DTW)-based K-means, HMM K-model, HMM hybrid clustering, HMM hybrid meta-clustering, and our approach on the benchmark collection, where the performance of the K-means algorithm is provided by benchmark collectors. The class number of each data set, K^*, used in the algorithms includes K-means, DTW-based K-means, HMM K-model, HMM hybrid clustering, and HMM hybrid meta-clustering. In contrast, there is not the user input of class number in our approach due to its automatic model-selection ability. For our approach, we did not use the information of the class number of each data set and simply select K value of cluster number

Table 5.3 Time Series Benchmark Information

Data Set	Number of Class K^*	Size of Data Set (Training + Testing)	Length
Syn control	6	300 ± 300	60
Gun point	2	50 ± 150	150
CBF	3	30 ± 900	128
Face (all)	14	560 ± 1690	131
OSU leaf	6	200 ± 242	427
Swedish leaf	15	500 ± 625	128
50 words	50	450 ± 455	270
Trace	4	100 ± 100	275
Two patterns	4	1000 ± 4000	128
Wafer	2	1000 ± 6174	152
Face (four)	4	24 ± 88	350
Lightning-2	2	60 ± 61	637
Lightning- 7	7	70 ± 73	319
ECG	2	100 ± 100	96
Adiac	37	390 ± 391	176
Yoga	2	300 ± 3000	426

from a preset range $K^* - 2 \leq K \leq K^* + 2$ $(K > 0)$. In order to compare model-selection ability based on our proposed DPSA consensus function with the standard model-selection approach, we also modified our approach with BIC model selection, which determines the optimal number of clusters from a range of clusters size, with a minimum value of BIC. For HMM-based clustering algorithms, the state number of HMM models are critical for the performance of modeling the time series. However, these information are not given for time series benchmarks. Therefore, we could only employ an exhaustive search to determine optimal number of states for each of data set included in the time series benchmarks, which are correspondingly 6,2,4,9,2,6,3,10,8,8,9,6,7,8,2,3.

Table 5.4 lists all the results achieved in this experiment. For each algorithm, we run the experiment 10 times with best parameter setup, and the best result is reported in the table. It is observed from Table 5.4 that there is not any algorithm that had had outstanding performance than others. Comparably, our approach outperforms other methods, as it has the best performance on 6 of 16 data sets. DTW-based K-means surprisingly achieves best results for five data sets, the HMM K-model, HMM hybrid clustering, and HMM hybrid meta-clustering algorithms win on two, one and two data sets, respectively. Given the fact that our approach based on both of BIC model selection and DSPA consensus function are capable for finding a cluster number in a given data set, we also report their model-selection performance with the notation that * is added behind the classification accuracy if the algorithm finds

Table 5.4 Classification Accuracy (%)[a] of Clustering Algorithms on Time Series Benchmarks

Data Set	K-Means	DTW-Based K-means	HMM K-Model	HMM Hybrid Clustering	HMM Hybrid Meta-Clustering	Our Approach (BIC Model Selection)	Our Approach
Syn control	67.9	69.8	69.1	69.8	71.1	70.8*	**73.2***
Gun point	50.0	**65.6**	43.8	51.8	50.0	56.0*	65.2*
CBF	62.6	**80.9**	60.1	63.2	65.2	70.0*	64.3*
Face (all)	36.0	**49.4**	37.8	36.4	39.2	23.6	31.4
OSU leaf	37.8	35.1	44.2	40.8	**45.1**	35.0	38.0
Swedish leaf	40.6	48.1	38.6	47.6	**49.2**	28.3	42.5*
50 words	42.0	37.2	40.8	38.9	41.0	39.1	**46.2***
Trace	48.5	63.4	50.9	56.3	59.8	61.8*	**63.9***
Two patterns	32.2	**56.3**	33.1	35.2	38.1	27.2	50.6*
Wafer	62.5	47.5	63.9	**65.1**	62.9	54.2*	53.4
Face (four)	66.9	**70.7**	69.1	64.2	61.9	49.7	58.8
Lightning-2	61.1	62.1	57.7	63.2	66.8	51.6	**67.6***
Lightning-7	48.4	50.5	**51.2**	47.3	45.3	49.5	50.0*
ECG	69.8	62.8	**70.3**	61.6	63.3	55.5	65.8
Adiac	38.4	39.6	38.9	42.0	40.2	38.9*	**43.2***
Yoga	51.7	56.3	48.5	44.3	47.1	34.8	**63.8***

[a] *Notation of correct cluster number determined*

the correct cluster numbers. As a result, our approach based on proposed DPSA consensus function is able to find the correct cluster number on 11 of 16 data sets, and BIC model-selection criteria manage to find the correct cluster number for six data sets only, as shown in Table 5.4. The results indicate the challenge of standard model-selection criteria such as BIC in clustering temporal data of high dimensions. However, our approach based on proposed DPSA consensus function achieves promising results in terms of model selection and proper grouping. It is worth mentioning that all HMM-based algorithms reported in the experiments take a much longer time in comparison with K-means algorithm. The computational burden becomes quite significant when applying HMM-based clustering algorithms on the temporal data set with large volume and high dimensionality, which would be a major weakness of such approachs.

5.3.4 MOTION TRAJECTORY

For evaluating our approach in the real-world application, we apply our approach to the CAVIAR database for trajectory clustering analysis. The CAVIAR database is a benchmark designed for video content analysis (CAVIAR, 2002). From the manually annotated video sequences of pedestrians, a set of 222 high-quality motion trajectories are achieved for clustering analysis without concerning the affection of a visual-tracking algorithm. Fig. 5.7 illustrates the collection of all the motion

FIGURE 5.7

All motion trajectories in the CAVIAR database.

trajectories in the database. A motion trajectory is a 2D spatiotemporal data of the notation $\{(x(t), y(t))\}_{t=1}^{T}$, where $(x(t), y(t))$ are the coordinates of an object tracked at frame t.

Given that there is no prior knowledge on the "right" number of HMM model states and clusters for this database, we manually determine the optimal state number as two by an exhaust search and run the HMM K-models as base leaner 10 times by choosing a K value from an interval between 5 and 10 with random HMM model initialization, then 10 partitions generated are fed to our clustering ensemble to yield three consensus partition candidates, finally the optimal consensus partition is obtained from three candidates by a refining process based on HMM-agglomerative clustering algorithm, and the optimal cluster number as eight in the final partition is automatically determined by proposed DPSA consensus function.

Without the ground truth, human visual inspection has to be applied for evaluating the results, as suggested in the study by Khalid and Naftel (2005). As observable in Fig. 5.8, coherent motion trajectories in a similar path have been properly grouped together while dissimilar ones are distributed into different clusters. From the camera viewpoint, the trajectories corresponding to "move horizontally" following the same path are grouped very well into a single cluster shown in Fig. 5.8A, while the "move vertically" trajectories at different location are grouped into two clusters shown in Fig. 5.8C and F. Trajectories corresponding to "walk and watch" movement are properly grouped into a single clusters, as shown in Fig. 5.8G. Fig. 5.8D–E indicate that trajectories corresponding to most activities of "enter and enter the store" are properly grouped together via multiple clusters in light of motion path. Finally, Fig. 5.8H illustrates the cluster roughly corresponding to the activity "pass in front". It is worth to mention that our approach is insensitive to distinguish the trajectories following a similar motion part with opposite direction. For example,

FIGURE 5.8

A clustering analysis of all moving trajectories on the CAVIAR database made by HMM-based meta-clustering ensemble model. Plots in A—H correspond to 8 clusters of moving trajectories in the final partition.

the trajectories corresponding to "move up" and "move down" are merged into same cluster of "move horizontally" shown in Fig. 5.8A, while "move left" and "move right" trajectories at different locations are grouped into two clusters of "move vertically" shown in Fig. 5.8C and F. However, results of the clustering analysis obtained by our approach still can be used to infer different activities based on the motion path at a semantic level.

As mentioned in the previous experiments, we experienced that the HMM-based clustering algorithms are quite time consuming, especially on the temporal data with large volume and high dimensionality. In order to compare the computational cost of HMM-based clustering ensemble with other proposed approaches presented in the latter chapters, we initially record the execution time of applying our proposed HMM-based clustering ensemble presented in this chapter on the CAVIAR database for trajectory clustering analysis, which results in 4623.44 s.

For further evaluation, we have performed one more additional experiment in classification by adding different amounts of Gaussian noise $N(0,\sigma)$, to the range of coordinates and removed five segments of trajectory of the identical length at random locations in order to simulate common scenarios that a moving object tracked is occluded by other objects or the background so that a tracking algorithm has to produce a trajectory with missing data and recorded that motion trajectory data are interfered by external noise. Corrupted trajectories are used for testing where a decision is made by finding a cluster whose corresponding HMM model represents the tested trajectory in terms of the maximum log-likelihood to see if its clean version belongs to this cluster. Apparently, the classification accuracy depends largely on the quality of clustering analysis. Fig. 5.9 shows performance evolution in the presence of missing data measured by a percentage of the trajectory length added

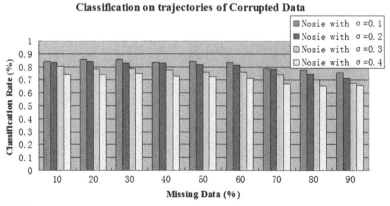

FIGURE 5.9

Performance of the HMM-based meta-clustering ensemble model on CAVIAR with corrupted data appears.

by different amounts of noise. It is evident that our approach performs well in real-world situations.

In summary, all the previously mentioned simulation results suggest that our model leads to robust clustering analysis. Therefore, the results may be used for higher level video content analyses.

5.4 SUMMARY

In this chapter, we have presented HMM-based hybrid meta-clustering in association with ensemble technique for temporal data. Based on our experimental results, we conclude that our proposed model yields robust clustering results and hence is suitable for application in an unknown environment, such as one with no prior information about the cluster number.

Essentially, our approach is proposed by modifying the HMM-based hierarchical meta-clustering described in previous Section 3.2.4 in order to overcome the problems of HMM model initialization sensitivity and selection of cluster number existed in the original approach. Therefore, our approach still inherent two major benefits from original approach by combining the strengths of partitioning and hierarchical approaches, which has been justified by Zhong and Ghosh (2003). First, no parameter re-estimation is required for the new merged pair of clusters which maximally reduces computation cost. As described in Section 3.2.2, the clusters of optimal consensus partition obtained from clustering ensemble are treated as meta-data, then standard HMM-based agglomerative clustering is applied to group the meta-data, where the distance between meta-data as intercluster distance is calculated and compared by using the symmetric version of BoundaryKL distance measure based on log-likelihood, the closest pair of clusters is merged to form a composite model concatenating the model parameters of each cluster instead of re-estimating the parameters of merged clusters. Second, the composite model is better equipped to characterize complexly structured clusters in comparison of single model such as HMM-based hybrid partitional-hierarchical clustering. The robust and accurate clustering performance obtained by our proposed approach has been demonstrated on various temporal data sets including HMM-generated data set shown in Table 5.1, a general synthetic data set (CBF) shown in Table 5.2, and a collection of time series benchmarks shown in Table 5.4. Moreover, our approach is also beneficial from insensitivity of HMM model initialization and automatic selection of cluster number by associating clustering ensemble techniques. As demonstrated in the early experiments by running each of clustering algorithms (HMM-K-models, HMM-agglomerative, HMM-divisive clustering, HMM-based hybrid clustering, HMM-based hybrid meta-clustering, and our approach) 10 times on the HMM-generated data set and CBF data set, our approach results the highest averaged classification rate, and the smallest valued standard deviation indicates that our approach is insensitive to the HMM model initialization in comparison of other HMM-based clustering algorithms. Furthermore, the experimental results reported in Table 5.4 demonstrate that DPSA consensus function involved in our approach obtains an efficient model-selection ability of automatically determining the cluster number; it is able to find the correct cluster number on 11 out of 16 data sets, which significantly outperforms BIC model-selection criteria that manage to find the correct cluster number for six data sets only.

However, there are some important open theoretical questions which must be considered. For model-based temporal data clustering, it is quite difficult to choose a suitable model family such as HMM, mixture of first-order Markov chain (Smyth, 1999), dynamic Bayesian networks (Murphy, 2002), or autoregressive moving average model (Xiong and Yeung, 2002), in terms of which it better represents differently structured temporal data without any prior information. For HMM-based clustering, the state emission probability is modeled as multivariate Gaussian. Here, how to select the number of Gaussian components for individual state emission function would come into question. In general terms, the multivariate Gaussian has been found to offer better performance than single Gaussian (Butler, 2003), but its use is limited for the considerable reasons of high computational demands and overfitting on the limited training data set available. On the other hand, how to determine the number of states would be critical for HMM model configuration. Moreover, the model-based clustering algorithms are usually combined with an EM algorithm for parameter estimation, even though the EM always causes the problems of local optima and convergence difficulty. For clustering algorithm, the algorithm efficiency is still a critical issue for temporal data with huge volume and high dimensionality, the computational cost of HMM-based clustering combining with ensemble techniques becomes even more expensive. As demonstrated on the CAVIAR database in simulation section, our approach is quite time consuming which could be a major limitation of applying our approach on the real-world or online applications. Therefore, how to find a tradeoff solution between computational cost and clustering performance becomes an urgent topic for model-based clustering.

Unsupervised Learning via an Iteratively Constructed Clustering Ensemble

6

CHAPTER OUTLINE

6.1 INTRODUCTION

Although clustering ensembles have been widely recognized as providing a effective method for improving robustness, stability, and accuracy in unsupervised classification or clustering tasks, they always incur high computational costs in terms of time and memory consumption. These may be trivial issues for clustering tasks based on small data sets, but for temporal data clustering, they become critical, for example, our proposed Hiddden Markov Model-based clustering ensemble model presented in the previous chapter suffer a major problem of time consumption. Therefore, a trade-off solution between clustering performance and computational efficiency must be sought. A clustering ensemble in asswith a subsampling technique can bring improvements to clustering performance in terms of both accuracy and computational efficiency.

Essentially, ensemble approaches can be summarized in two categories. In the first (Strehl and Ghosh, 2003; Fred and Jain, 2005; Viswanath and Jayasurya, 2006), all independent ensemble members (partitions) on the training set are generated in parallel and the optimal solution is obtained by combining multiple partitions into a single consensus partition. However, the major disadvantage of this approach is the lack of interaction among individual partitions. For example, the generated multiple partitions are highly biased toward similar clustering structures, which may not be useful enough to improve the clustering performance.

Temporal Data Mining via Unsupervised Ensemble Learning. http://dx.doi.org/10.1016/B978-0-12-811654-8.00006-3

Therefore, variances such as bagging (Dudoit and Fridlyand, 2003; Fischer and Buhmann, 2003) are introduced in order to increase the diversity of multiple input partitions during the procedure of initial clustering analysis by bootstrapping the training set. In contrast, the second category of ensemble approaches, such as boosting (Frossyniotis et al., 2004; Pavlovic, 2004; Liu et al., 2007; Saffari and Bischof, 2007), provides a new iterative approach creating a meaningful combination of sequentially constructed partitions which deals with the hard-clustered data points in the previous iteration through the use of a "smart" weighting scheme.

Although much of the literature (Dudoit and Fridlyand, 2003; Fischer and Buhmann, 2003; Monti et al., 2003; Strehl and Ghosh, 2003; Weingessel et al., 2003; Frossyniotis et al., 2004; Fred and Jain, 2005; Viswanath and Jayasurya, 2006; Gionis et al., 2007; Liu et al., 2007; Saffari and Bischof, 2007; Singh et al., 2007) shows improved performance of those ensemble approaches in terms of robustness and quality of clustering tasks, each still has its own limitations. For instance, bagging introduces randomness in the production of diverse multiple input partitions, but without a proper objective, it improves clustering performance purely by chance. On the other hand, boosting adjusts the sample weights by using clustering error, which is determined by an objective function based on certain clustering quality measurements, in spite of the fact that clustering quality measurements are often unilateral and biased toward certain cluster structure.

In this chapter, we present a novel ensemble approach to iteratively construct an ensemble of partitions generated on subsets sampled from the original data set through a hybrid sampling scheme. The approach is inspired by both boosting and bagging techniques originally proposed for supervised learning tasks. Our approach combines the strengths of both boosting and bagging approaches while attempting to avoid their drawbacks. It has been applied on a set of synthetic and real-world data sets. Simulation results indicate that such approach yields favorable performance in general clustering tasks.

The rest of this chapter is organized as follows: Firstly, we discuss the most common clustering ensemble approaches related to this work, including both bagging and boosting, and then describe the motivation behind the proposed model. Subsequently, simulation results for a variety of clustering tasks are reported. A summary concludes this chapter.

6.2 ITERATIVELY CONSTRUCTED CLUSTERING ENSEMBLE

In this section, we provide a brief analysis of boosting and bagging, as they relate to proposed clustering ensemble approach, and then describe the motivation for proposing the model. Finally, the algorithm description presents the proposed clustering ensemble model.

6.2.1 MOTIVATION

For both of boosting and bagging, we can observe that the major difference between the approaches is their respective sampling schemes determining their own behaviors, which in turn creates both advantages and disadvantages in dealing with various structured data for clustering tasks.

The randomness introduced by the sampling scheme in bagging creates no guarantees for the performance of a clustering task. Furthermore, if there is a large data set, it is impossible to see the whole training set due to the computational cost. In such instance, a sampling scheme based on the bootstrap with replicates of the training set becomes unfeasible. Instead, we can apply the subsampling approach to generate the training sample, although this alternative often cancels out any gains achieved by a bagging ensemble.

Although the outstanding performance of boosting in classification tasks gives strong motivation for extending it as an unsupervised learning approach. it is not easy to develop a boosting algorithm for clustering as there is no ground truth for guiding learning procedure. There also remain some critical issues that have to be addressed. First, instance weights driven from clustering quality measures such as the objective function always emphasize the unilateral aspects of clustering quality, which differs from classification tasks that associate with ground truth as objective criteria. Thus, the instances weighting scheme may not be trustworthy. Second, for multiple partitions, the ordering of cluster labels is arbitrary, and it is not meaningful to compare such cluster labels resulted in multiple partitions. This is referred to as a cluster-correspondence problem. Finally, boosting is sensitive to noise and unbalanced clustered structure, which can cause some "important" instances to lose their opportunity to be trained.

In response, we believe that a hybrid sampling scheme derived from these ensemble approaches, where part of the subset is selected by a weighting scheme based on boosting with the rest of the set randomly picked up with a bagging approach, may combine each of their strengths while compensating for each of their weaknesses. In order to achieve a visual inspection on the demonstration, this idea is illustrated by the following example.

As illustrated in Fig. 6.1A, there is a two-dimensional synthetic data set which is subjected to a mixture of Gaussian distribution where there are five intrinsic clusters of heterogeneous structures. The ground-truth partition is given for evaluation and marked by green triangle (cluster 1), red circle (cluster 2), cyan square (cluster 3), red cross (cluster 4), and blue dot (cluster 5). A visual interpretation of the structure of the data set shown in Fig. 6.1 suggests that while clusters 1 and 2 are relatively separate, cluster 3 spreads widely and clusters 4 and 5 of different populations overlap each other.

Without any sampling approaches, we initially apply the single K-means algorithm on the whole data set and a simple clustering ensemble that combines 10 partitions obtained by running K-means with different restarts on the whole data set into a single partition based on the linear combination, while other ensemble algorithms with corresponding sampling approaches are also applied by using K-means

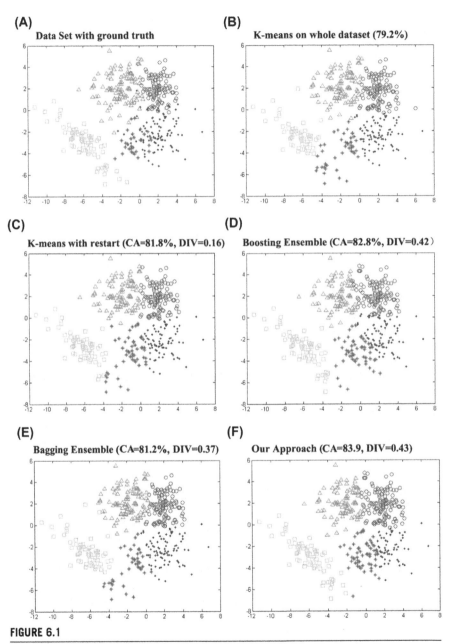

FIGURE 6.1

Results of various clustering approaches on synthetic data set with classification accuracy.

as base learner, where 10 partitions obtained from the subsampled training set (sampling rate, $\gamma = 0.1$) are combined into a single partition based on the linear combination.

By visual inspection, we evaluate the clustering quality of each method. All methods can well identify clusters 1 and 2 illustrated in Fig. 6.1B—F. With regard to the whole data set, Fig. 6.1B and C shows that the K-means and clustering ensemble based on restart K-means still fails to fully separate clusters 3—5, with a classification accuracy of 79.2% and 81.8% separately. Boosting attempts to focus on the hard-clustered instances to recycle the subtraining set sampled from this region by a weighting scheme. This produces a slightly better result in comparison with single K-means and clustering ensemble based on restart K-means, which gives a classification accuracy of 82.8%, as shown in Fig. 6.1D. However, the weighting scheme derived from a clustering quality measurement based only on cluster compactness and separability does not adapt to a complex cluster structure. In this structure, clusters 4 and 5 (of different populations) overlap each other and, in a few instances, belong to the manifold shape in cluster 3 at the bottom of Fig. 6.1D, which is set apart from the dense region of data points. As illustrated in Fig. 6.1D, part of cluster 4, cluster 5, and a few of the outliers in cluster 3 are improperly grouped together due to overtraining on this region by boosting. Bagging gives each instance an equal opportunity to be trained by a random sampling approach and combines the parallel generated partitions based on majority voting. This is more likely to result in clusters of a balanced structure. As illustrated in Fig. 6.1E, bagging is able to separate clusters 4 and 5 but fails to group cluster 3 where part of cluster 3 is merged into cluster 4, achieving a classification accuracy of 81.2%. In contrast, our proposed clustering ensemble partly adds random sampling based on bagging to weight-based sampling based on boosting, where part of the subtraining set ($\eta = 0.5$) is obtained by boosting sampling schema and the rest of the subtraining set ($1 - \eta$) is constructed using random sampling from the input space based on bagging ensemble approach, thereby building up a hybrid sampling scheme. This significantly reduces biases caused by a weighting scheme based on the unilateral clustering quality measurement and also maintains the gains of bagging, which is insensitive to the noise data. Fig. 6.1F demonstrates an outstanding performance of our proposed approach in comparison to other methods.

Studies (Brown et al., 2002; Kuncheva and Whitaker, 2003; Kuncheva and Hadjitodorov, 2004) have indicated that more diversity offers larger improvement on the clustering ensemble than less diversity. In other words, higher diversity among ensemble members more likely produces higher clustering performance gain in the final consensus partition, and the diversity of clustering ensemble can be obtained by several manners. In this case, we mainly focus on combining different clustering results by sampling data to produce a final single result. Actually there are a number of different ways to measure the diversity of ensemble members including Rand Index, Jaccard Index, Adjusted Rand Index, Normalized Mutual Information (NMI) (Hadjitodorov et al., 2006). Most of them are based on label matching between two partitions, where two partitions are to be diverse if the labels of one partition do not match well with the labels of the other. One diversity measure (DIV) commonly used in the literature is the NMI, which is formulated as following:

$$
\text{NMI}(P_a, P_b) = \frac{\sum_{i=1}^{K_a} \sum_{j=1}^{K_b} N_{ij}^{ab} \log\left(\frac{N N_{ij}^{ab}}{N_i^a N_j^b}\right)}{\sum_{i=1}^{K_a} N_i^a \log\left(\frac{N_i^a}{N}\right) + \sum_{j=1}^{K_b} N_j^b \log\left(\frac{N_j^b}{N}\right)} \tag{6.1}
$$

$$
\text{DIV} = 1 - \frac{2}{T(T-1)} \sum_{i=1}^{T-1} \sum_{j=i+1}^{T} \text{NMI}(P_i, P_j) \tag{6.2}
$$

where a set of T input partitions $P = \{P_t\}_{t=1}^{T}$ obtained from a target data set, P_i, $P_j \in P$. DIV based on NMI is valued from 0 to 1, the higher value represents a collection of more diverse ensemble members obtained from the target data set. In order to explore the relation between diversity of clustering ensemble and performance based on classification accuracy, we further apply NMI-based DIV among the ensemble members obtained from different clustering algorithms. As illustrated in Fig. 6.1, the sampling-based clustering ensemble algorithms including boosting, bagging, and our approach produces much more diverse partitions with DIV value (0.42, 0.37, 0.43) shown in Fig. 6.1D–F. In contrast, the clustering ensemble produces less diversity among the input partitions obtained by applying K-means with restart on the whole training data set, which gives a DIV value of 0.16 shown in Fig. 6.1C. It is obvious that the restart K-means-based clustering ensemble results in a higher classification accuracy with lower DIV value than bagging ensemble, which produces an inconsistent relation between diversity and performance for clustering ensemble. Therefore, we believe that the diversity among ensemble members still cannot be solely used as main factor to judge the performance of clustering ensemble, which has been mentioned in Section 4.4. However, the partition yielded by our proposed model is very close to the ground truth in Fig. 6.1A with the highest classification accuracy of 83.9% and DIV value of 0.43, strongly encouraging the development of an iteratively constructed clustering ensemble with a novel sampling scheme.

6.2.2 MODEL DESCRIPTION

Based on the motivation described previously, we propose a sampling-based clustering ensemble approach; an iteratively constructed clustering ensemble. This approach iteratively constructs the multiple partitions on the subset of whole input instances selected by a hybrid of boosting and bagging sampling schemes as illustrated in Fig. 6.2. At each iteration, weights over instances are updated, part of the subset defined by the fraction parameter η is chosen according to the weights over instances as a selection probability, and the rest of the subset $(1 - \eta)$ is constructed using random sampling from the input data set. Then, a clustering algorithm

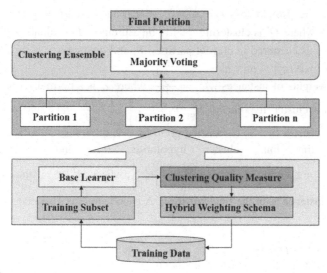

FIGURE 6.2

Iteratively constructed clustering ensemble (Yang and Chen, 2010).

such as K-means is applied to partition the subsets in order to generate several partitions, then the partitions are combined into a final result using a majority voting, where the weights of the partition measure the clustering quality. The detailed algorithm description is given as follows:

1. Set all instance weights equal, $W^t = \{w_i^t\}_{i=1}^N = 1/N$ and $t = 1$.
2. Produce a training set consisting of two parts from the original data set. One part of training set with higher weights are selected by boosting sampling schema, the rest of training set are randomly selected by bagging sampling schema.
3. Given a predefined clustering number K*, K-means is applied as a base learner on the training set in order to produce a partition P_t.
4. Get the cluster hypothesis, $H_i^t = \left(h_{i,1}^t, h_{i,2}^t, \ldots, h_{i,k*}^t\right)$ for each of instance, where $h_{i,j}^t$ is a membership degree of instance x_i to cluster $C_j^t \in P_t$. It is defined as

$$h_{i,j}^t = \frac{1}{\sum_{k=1}^{K^*} \frac{d(x_i,\mu_j)}{d(x_i,\mu_k)}},$$ where $d(x_i,\mu_j)$ and $d(x_i,\mu_k)$ are Euclidean distance between

instance x_i and centers (μ_j, μ_k) of cluster $(C_j^t \in P_t, C_k^t \in P_t)$, respectively.

5. Form an $N \times K^*$ cluster hypothesis, $H^t = \left[h_{i,j}^t\right]_{i=1,\ldots,N; \, j=1,\ldots,K^*}$ for whole data set. If $t > 1$, renumber the cluster indexes of H^t using the aggregate hypothesis, H_{ag}^{t-1}, in the previous iteration for cluster-correspondence problem by Hungarian algorithm (Winston and Goldberg, 1994). Otherwise, go directly to Step 6.

6. Compute the pseudo loss $\varepsilon_t = \frac{1}{2} \sum_{i=1}^{N} w_i^t Q_i^t$ and set current partition weight $\beta_t = \frac{1-\varepsilon_t}{\varepsilon_t}$, where Q_i^t is clustering quality measurement to evaluate how well an instance x_i is clustered in current partition P_t and defined as $Q_i^t = 1 - \max(h_i^t) - \min(h_i^t)$.

7. Update weights of instances $w_i^{t+1} = \frac{w_i^t \beta_t^{Q_i^t}}{Z_t}$, where Z_t is a normalization constant

8. Aggregate cluster hypothesis $H_{ag}^t = \sum_{\tau=1}^{t} \left[\frac{\log(\beta_\tau)}{\sum_{j=1}^{t} \log(\beta_j)} H^\tau \right]$ and $t = t + 1$. If stopping criteria $(t > T)$ is satisfied go to Step 9, otherwise go to Step 2.

9. Output the final cluster hypothesis H_{ag}^T and final partition $H_{ag}^T(x_i) = \arg\max_{k=1,\ldots,K^*} \sum_{t=1}^{T} \left[\frac{\log(\beta_t)}{\sum_{j=1}^{T} \log(\beta_j)} h_{i,k}^t \right]$, where $H_{ag}^T(x_i)$ is the cluster label of instance x_i in the final partition. A pseudocode is also given

Input:

- *a data set $X = \{x_1, x_2, \ldots, x_N\}$.*
- *an integer K^* (intrinsic cluster number)*
- *an integer T (number of iterations)*
- *an integer γ (sampling rate)*
- *an integer η (fraction rate)*
- *the K-means clustering algorithm KM*
- *the Euclidean distance function d*
- *the Hungarian algorithm HUNGARIAN*

Initialize $W^t = \{w_i^t\}_{i=1}^{N} = 1/N$, set $t = 1$
while $t \leq T$
   Produce a training set consisting of two parts from the
   original dataset:
   $|X_{training}| = \gamma|X|$
   $X_{training} = \{X_{boosting}, X_{bagging}\}$
   $X_{boosting}$ is selected according to instance weights W^t (Boosting sampling)
   $X_{bagging}$ is randomly selected (Bagging sampling)
   $|X_{training}| = \eta|X_{boosting}| + (1 - \eta)|X_{bagging}|$
   $P_t = Kmeans(X_{training}, K^*)$
   for $i = 1$ to N
     for $j = 1$ to K^*
      $h_{i,j}^t = \dfrac{1}{\sum_{k=1}^{K^*} \dfrac{d(x_i, \mu_j)}{d(x_i, \mu_k)}}$; //$\mu_j = \overline{X}_{C_j^t}$ and $\mu_k = \overline{X}_{C_k^t}$ (cluster j and k in

               //partition P_t, $C_j^t \in P_t$, $C_k^t \in P_t$)

     end for
   end for
   $H^t = [h_{i,j}^t]_{N \times K^*}$;
   if $t > 1$

$$H^t = HUNGARIAN\left(H^t, H_{ag}^{t-1}\right);$$

end if

$$Q_i^t = 1 - \max_i\left(h_i^t\right) - \min\left(h_i^t\right); \ \varepsilon_t = \tfrac{1}{2}\sum_{i=1}^N w_i^t Q_i^t; \ \beta_t = \tfrac{1-\varepsilon_t}{\varepsilon_t};$$

$$w_i^{t+1} = \tfrac{w_i^t \beta_t^{-i}}{Z_t}; \textit{// } Z_t \textit{ is a normalization constant}$$

$$H_{ag}^t = \sum_{\tau=1}^t \left[\frac{\log(\beta_\tau)}{\sum_{j=1}^t \log(\beta_j)}H^\tau\right]; \ t = t+1$$

end while

$$H_{ag}^T = H_{ag}^t$$

Output: the final partition $H_{ag}^T(x_i) = \arg \max_{k=1,\ldots,K^*} \sum_{t=1}^T \left[\frac{\log(\beta_t)}{\sum_{j=1}^T \log(\beta_j)}h_{i,k}^t\right],$ *where*

$H_{ag}^T(x_i)$ *is the cluster label of instance* x_i *in the final partition.*

6.3 SIMULATION

In this section, we present our experimental methodology and simulation results. Although the outcome of clustering analysis can be used for miscellaneous tasks, we focus only on clustering-based classification tasks in simulations. We apply the proposed ensemble approach to a synthetic time series—Cylinder-Bell-Funnel, a collection of 16 synthetic or real-world time series data sets (Keogh, 2003), and motion trajectories database (CAVIAR, 2002). In the following section, we report the performance of our model in three benchmark clustering tasks.

6.3.1 CYLINDER-BELL-FUNNEL DATA SET

This data set consists of three classes of data, cylinder (c), bell (b), or funnel (f). They are already used for evaluating the proposed HMM-based hybrid meta-clustering ensemble model presented in the previous chapter. The details of the data set have been described in Section 5.3.2. For comparison, we employ five algorithms on this synthetic data. First, we apply K-means on the whole data set as a baseline, as well as a clustering ensemble algorithm achieved by applying restart K-means on the whole data set with the correct number of clusters ($K = 3$). Then, both boosting and bagging clustering ensemble approaches are implemented while K-means remains as the base learner. Given the fact that both ensemble approaches were developed without addressing model selection, we also use the correct number of clusters ($K = 3$) in K-means, while the best parameter setup ($\gamma = 0.1$, $\eta = 0.5$) are given for our approach. Thus, 10 partitions generated are combined by different ensemble approaches. For our approach, we use exactly the same procedure for K-means to produce partitions on the subset with the hybrid sampling scheme described earlier. After visual inspection, we represent the best clustering results obtained by these algorithms in the original time domain illustrated in Fig. 6.3B–F. It is observed from Fig. 6.3B that the whole data set can be seen, and K-means still presents significant challenges in directly performing clustering analysis on high-dimensional data such as time series, achieving a classification accuracy of 61.1%. On the other hand, by using the same K-means algorithms as base learners, restarting K-means-based clustering ensemble without sampling on the whole

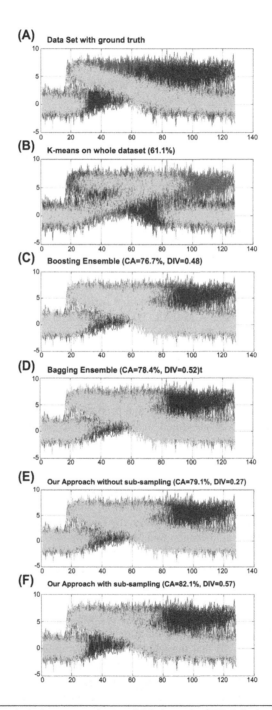

FIGURE 6.3

Results of various clustering approaches on CBF data set. *CBF*, Cylinder-Bell-Funnel; *DIV*, diversity measure.

dataset and both boosting and bagging ensemble approaches with the corresponding sampling techniques obtain better clustering results (79.1, 76.7%, and 78.4%). However, due to the sampling techniques, the boosting and bagging clustering ensemble algorithms produces much more diversity among the ensemble members, which is evaluated by an NMI-based DIV (0.48, 0.52) shown in Fig. 6.1D and E than clustering ensemble achieved by applying K-means with restart on the whole data set, which results DIV = 0.27 shown in Fig. 6.1B. As illustrated in Fig. 6.3F, the proposed approach with a hybrid sampling on the whole data set produces much more diverse input partitions (DIV = 0.53), which gives more opportunity that input partitions capture a significant amount of different features based on the intrinsic cluster structure from different perspectives. As a result, it achieves the best performance based on classification accuracy of 82.1% where the final partition yielded by our proposed model is very close to the ground truth in Fig. 6.3A in comparison with the other four algorithms.

Furthermore, we examine the performance of our approach using different values of η. As illustrated in Fig. 6.4, the average classification accuracy of our approach varies with the input parameter without any regularity. In fact, additional experiments, not reported here, have been performed in order to explore the nature of subtraining set fraction parameter λ on different data sets. Based on the results, we realize that is extremely difficult to establish a general framework to determine the optimal value of this input parameter on various data sets, which would be an open question for future research.

6.3.2 TIME SERIES BENCHMARKS

For investigating the performance of ensemble learning, we further apply the proposed iteratively constructed clustering ensemble associated various static clustering algorithms (Hierarchical clustering, K-NN, and K-means) as base learner and relative clustering ensemble algorithms (boosting and bagging) on time series benchmarks of 16

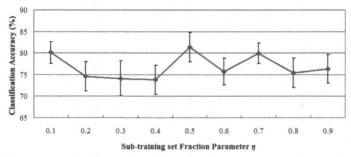

FIGURE 6.4

Performance of iteratively constructed clustering ensemble model on subtraining set fraction parameter η (Yang and Chen, 2010).

synthetic or real-world time series data sets (Keogh, 2003), previously used in Chapter 5 for evaluating our proposed HMM-based clustering ensemble model. The information on all 16 data sets has been presented in Section 5.3.3.

In this experiment, we also use a whole data set by merging training and testing subsets for the evaluation of clustering algorithms. Given the fact that these ensemble approaches were developed without addressing model selection, the correct cluster number is given for the initial clustering analysis and the optimal parameter setup invoked in our approach is manually determined by an exhausted search, which is shown in Table 6.1 for each of time series benchmarks.

Table 6.2 lists all the results achieved in this experiment. For each algorithm, we run the experiment 10 times with best parameter setup, and the best result is reported in the table, where the performance of the K-means algorithm is provided by benchmark collectors. It is observed from Table 6.2 that our approach associated with three different basic clustering algorithms as base learner, all achieves the promising results, as it has the best performance on 14 of 16 data sets in comparison with other clustering algorithms, where the K-means, boosting ensemble clustering, and bagging ensemble clustering algorithms only win on one, zero, and one data sets, respectively. For comparison between different clustering algorithms as base learner invoked in our proposed iteratively constructed clustering ensemble, the results reported in the last three columns of Table 6.2 are quite even, where there is not any algorithm that had had outstanding performance than others. Comparably, K-means-based approach outperforms other methods, as it has the best performance on 6 out

Table 6.1 Optimal Parameter Setup of Our Approach on Time Series Benchmarks

Data Set	Number of Clusters (K*)	Sampling Rate (γ)	Sub-Training Set Fraction Rate (λ)
Syn control	6	0.50	0.50
Gun-point	2	0.20	0.25
CBF	3	0.50	0.50
Face (all)	14	0.50	0.50
OSU leaf	6	0.33	0.33
Swedish leaf	15	0.50	0.50
50 words	50	0.50	0.50
Trace	4	0.50	0.50
Two patterns	4	0.50	0.50
Wafer	2	0.50	0.50
Face (four)	4	0.50	0.50
Lightning-2	2	0.20	0.50
Lightning-7	7	0.50	0.83
ECG	2	0.33	0.50
Adiac	37	0.83	0.25
Yoga	2	0.17	0.17

Table 6.2 Classification Accuracy (%) of Clustering Algorithms on Time Series Benchmarks

Data Set	K-means	Bagging	Boosting	Our Approach (HIE)	Our Approach (K-NN)	Our Approach (K-means)
Syn control	67.9	70.7	73.0	60.8	71.0	**74.3**
Gun-point	50.0	50.0	65.1	**69.2**	57.3	56.7
CBF	62.6	64.2	64.3	66.2	**69.4**	64.8
Face (all)	36.0	39.2	38.9	34.0	40.1	**40.4**
OSU leaf	37.8	39.1	39.3	38.6	**43.3**	41.8
Swedish Leaf	40.6	43.5	41.6	32.0	**45.7**	44.6
50 words	42.0	42.4	39.0	**43.2**	39.4	40.9
Trace	48.5	52.5	52.9	50.6	**53.9**	53.5
Two patterns	32.2	33.2	32.4	**34.4**	33.3	33.2
Wafer	62.5	62.5	62.7	62.7	**63.6**	62.5
Face (four)	**66.9**	63.4	66.1	61.2	62.8	64.0
Lightning-2	61.1	62.9	64.8	63.1	64.6	**68.6**
Lightning-7	48.4	46.5	43.2	**50.9**	45.3	50.0
ECG	69.8	69.8	**76.5**	72.7	72.4	72.0
Adiac	38.4	40.8	37.2	24.6	43.8	**44.4**
Yoga	51.7	50.5	50.9	50.1	51.4	**51.9**

of 16 data sets. Hierarchical clustering and K-NN as base learner achieves best results for five data sets. As a result, we believe that our approach provides a more general framework for ensemble learning, where most of conventional clustering algorithms can be used as a base learner.

6.3.3 MOTION TRAJECTORY

In order to explore a potential application, we apply our approach to the CAVIAR database for trajectory clustering analysis. The CAVIAR database (CAVIAR, 2002) was previously used in Chapter 5 for evaluating the proposed HMM-based clustering ensemble model.

Motion trajectories tend to have various lengths, and therefore, a normalization technique would be required to unify the various lengths of motion trajectories. In this experiment, the motion trajectory is resampled with a prespecified number of sample points (1500) by a polynomial interpolation algorithm. After resampling, all trajectories are normalized to a Gaussian distribution of zero mean and unit variance in x and y directions. It is different from previous experiments presented in Section 5.3.4, the motion trajectories as 2D time series data of the notation $\{(x(t), y(t))\}_{t=1}^{T}$, where $(x(t), y(t))$ are the coordinates of an object tracked at frame t, are represented by concatenating two time series corresponding to its x and y projection into single dimensional time series in this simulation which are shown in Fig. 6.5.

In our simulation, the proposed approach is applied to all trajectories for clustering analysis. Since information on the "right" number of clusters is unavailable, we run the K-means algorithm 10 times on a subset of the training set by manually choosing a K value of 14 generating 10 partitions that are fed to the proposed ensemble model in order to yield a final partition with user-defined input parameter ($\eta = 0.35$), as shown in Fig. 6.6. Without the ground truth, human visual inspection has to be applied for evaluating the results, as suggested (Khalid and Naftel, 2005).

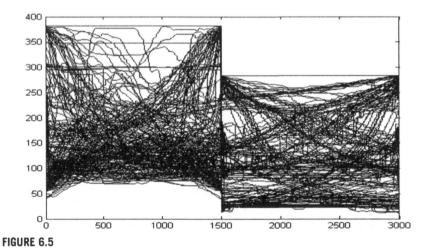

FIGURE 6.5

Preprocessed trajectories in the CAVIAR database.

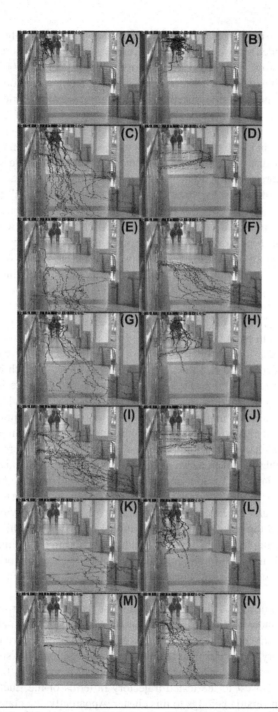

FIGURE 6.6

A clustering analysis of all moving trajectories on the CAVIAR database made by iteratively constructed clustering ensemble model. Plots in A–N correspond to 14 clusters of moving trajectories in the final partition (Yang and Chen, 2010).

Using common visual experience, behaviors of pedestrians across the shopping mall are roughly divided into five categories from the camera viewpoint: "move up," "move down," "stop," "move left," and "move right" (CAVIAR, 2002). Ideally, trajectories of similar behaviors are grouped together along a motion direction, and then results of clustering analysis are used to infer different activities at a semantic level, for example, "enter the store," "exit from the store," "pass in front," and "stop to watch."

As observable in Fig. 6.6, coherent motion trajectories have been properly grouped together while dissimilar ones are distributed into different clusters. For example, the trajectories corresponding to the activity of "stop to watch" are accurately grouped in the cluster shown in Fig. 6.6A, while the "walk and watch" trajectories are grouped into the cluster shown in Fig. 6.6M. Trajectories corresponding to movement from left-to-right and right-to-left are properly grouped into two separate clusters, as shown in Fig. 6.6D and J. Trajectories corresponding to "move up" and "move down" are grouped very well into two clusters as shown in Fig. 6.6C and G. Fig. 6.6B, F, H, I, L, and N indicate that trajectories corresponding to most activities of "enter the store" and "exit from the store" are properly grouped together via multiple clusters in light of various starting positions, locations, moving directions, and so on. Finally, Fig. 6.6E and K illustrate two clusters roughly corresponding to the activity "pass in front."

As mentioned in the Chapter 5, the former algorithm (HMM-based clustering ensemble) revealed a major problem of computational cost, which becomes much more critical for real-world application such as performing clustering analysis on CAVIAR database of motion trajectories (execution time, 4623.44s). In order to improve the algorithm efficiency, we intuitively proposed a new approach as the iteratively constructed clustering ensemble associated with a hybrid sampling technique presented in this chapter. For comparison of computational cost resulting in both proposed ensemble approaches, we also monitor the duration of clustering analysis on the CAVIAR database by applying the ensemble model presented in this chapter. Surprisingly, it is round 377 times faster than HMM-based clustering ensemble approach and results an execution time of only 12.27 seconds, which sufficiently demonstrates that the reduction of computational costs can be achieved by several manners, for example, implementing a simple clustering algorithm such as K-means as base learner, a simple consensus function such as majority voting, and reducing the training set by subsampling on the whole data set for ensemble learning approach.

To simulate trajectories of corrupted data in the real-world environment, we have performed one more additional experiment in classification by adding different amounts of Gaussian noise $N(0,\sigma)$, to the range of coordinates and removed five segments of trajectory of the identical length at random locations. Missing segments of various lengths are used for testing where a decision is made by finding a cluster whose center is closest to the tested trajectory in terms of the Euclidean distance to see if its clean version belongs to this cluster. Apparently, the classification accuracy depends largely on the quality of clustering analysis. Fig. 6.7 shows

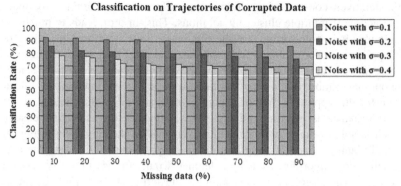

FIGURE 6.7

Performance of the iteratively constructed clustering ensemble model on CAVIAR with corrupted data appears (Yang and Chen, 2010).

performance evolution in the presence of missing data measured by a percentage of the trajectory length added by different amounts of noise. It is evident that our approach performs well in real-world situations.

In summary, all the previously mentioned simulation results suggest that our model leads to robust clustering analysis. Therefore, the results may be used for higher level video-content analyses.

6.4 SUMMARY

In this chapter, we have presented an unsupervised learning model for clustering tasks by using an ensemble of iteratively constructed partitions on the subtraining set obtained by a hybrid sampling scheme. Simulation results on different types of data sets demonstrate that our model yields favorable results. The experiments based on a set of synthetic and real data sets have justified the legitimacy of the fundamental concept behind our proposed approach. For real-world applications, the robustness and feasibility have been further evaluated using the motion video trajectory data set.

A similar ensemble algorithm (Kotsiantis and Pintelas, 2004) has also been developed for supervised learning. It combines two subensembles obtained by bagging and boosting on the same training set into a single classifier with sum rule voting in a parallel procedure. Although this algorithm uses similar ideas to those used in the construction of our algorithm, the classifiers are individually gener-ated by bagging and boosting resulting in a lack of interaction between these clas-sifiers. Furthermore, this algorithm would be unfeasible for large data sets due to high computational cost. In contrast, our algorithm develops a hybrid sampling scheme maximizing the synergy between bagging and boosting for clustering tasks, and the iteratively constructed partitions on the subtraining set significantly improve the interaction of multiple clustering solutions. This, in turn, leads to much faster computation. It is noteworthy that the efficiency issue is critical for some real-world applications, for example, temporal data and large data set clustering.

There are several issues to be studied in the ongoing research. First, the selection of the optimal number of clusters continues to pose a well-known model-selection problem for this approach. Without being given this a priori information, a rather poor performance is always produced. Next, although the clustering ensemble approach is able to make significant improvements on the single clustering algorithm and obtains a trade-off solution for arbitrary-structured data sets, the appropriate clustering algorithm as a base learner would further optimize clustering performance. Therefore, selection of a proper clustering algorithm for certain characterized data could be a further research topic. Finally, we released the proposed clustering ensemble model that has the major difficulties of dealing with the data sets with various lengths, which requires the data sets to be of uniform length, and combining the input partitions with different number of clusters due to the limitation of majority voting combination.

Temporal Data Clustering via a Weighted Clustering Ensemble With Different Representations

7

7.1 INTRODUCTION

As presented in previous chapters, proximity and model-based clustering approaches directly work on temporal data where temporal correlation is dealt directly during clustering analysis by means of temporal similarity measures (Jain et al., 1999; Keogh and Kasetty, 2003; Xu and Wunsch, 2005; Ding et al., 2008), for example, dynamic-time warping or dynamic models (Smyth, 1999; Policker and Geva, 2000; Murphy, 2002; Xiong and Yeung, 2002; Liu and Brown, 2004), for example, hidden Markov model (HMM). As presented in Chapter 5, a model-based approach, *HMM-based meta-clustering ensemble*, has been initially proposed in order to mainly solve problems in finding the intrinsic number of clusters and model initialization problems. However, it is quite time consuming, especially for the temporal data with huge volume and high dimensionality. Therefore, a proximity-based approach, *Iteratively constructed clustering ensemble*, presented in Chapter 6 has been proposed in order to reduce the computational cost and provide a meaningful combination of input partitions by a hybrid sampling technique. However, it strictly requires the prior number of clusters, the data sets with uniform length, and input partitions resulting in identical number of clusters. In order to solve the problems existed in both proposed clustering ensemble models, we consider that a feature-based approach would be an alternative solution.

Basically, a feature-based approach attends to convert temporal data into a lower dimensionality in feature space. Here, temporal data clustering supports the use of any static data–clustering algorithm, creating high computational efficiency. In the last 20 years, numerous representations have been proposed for temporal data clustering (Faloutsos et al., 1994; Dimitrova and Golshani, 1995; Chen and Chang, 2000; Keogh et al., 2001; Chakrabarti et al., 2002; Bagnall and Janacek, 2004; Bashir, 2005; Cheong et al., 2005; Bagnall et al., 2006; Gionis et al., 2007; Ding et al., 2008; Ye and Keogh, 2009). Nevertheless, one representation tends to encode only those features well presented in its representation space, which inevitably causes the loss of other useful information conveyed in the original temporal data. Due to the high complexity and varieties of temporal data, to our knowledge, there is no universal representation that perfectly characterizes miscellaneous temporal data. Therefore, a representation is merely applicable to a class of temporal data where their salient features can be fully captured in the representation space, but such information is hardly available without prior knowledge and a careful analysis. Furthermore, the aforementioned model-selection problem is still unavoidable, which is independent of the use of a representation.

In Section 4.5, we described in depth the essence of the clustering ensemble: a data set is subjected to a multiple partition combination in the expectation of producing a consensus partition superior to that of the given input partitions. Growing empirical evidence supports such a concept, indicating new cluster structures that the clustering ensemble is capable of detecting. Moreover, analyses reveal that under certain conditions, a consensus solution will in fact uncover the intrinsic underlying structure of a given data set (Topchy et al., 2004). These are strong, generic techniques enabling the joint use of different representations in temporal data clustering.

In response to the previously mentioned data and building on previous successes with different representations in complex pattern classification tasks (Chen et al., 1997; Chen, 1998; Chen and Chi, 1998; Chen, 2005a,b; Wang and Chen, 2007), this chapter presents an approach which can overcome weaknesses inherent in representation-based temporal data–clustering analysis. Our approach consists of initial clustering analysis on different representations to produce multiple partitions and clustering ensemble construction to produce a final partition by combining those partitions achieved in initial clustering analysis. While initial clustering analysis can be done by any existing clustering algorithms, we propose a novel weighted clustering ensemble (WCE) algorithm of a two-stage reconciliation process. In the proposed algorithm, a weighting consensus function reconciles input partitions to candidate consensus partitions according to various clustering validation criteria.

Then, an agreement function yields the final partition by further reconciling the candidate consensus partitions.

The contributions of this work are summarized as follows. First, we develop a practical temporal data clustering model by different representations via clustering ensemble learning to overcome the fundamental weakness in the representation-based temporal data—clustering analysis. Next, we propose a novel WCE algorithm, which not only provides an enabling technique to support our model but also can be used to combine any input partitions. Finally, we demonstrate the effectiveness and the efficiency of our model for a variety of temporal data clustering tasks as well as its easy-to-use nature as all internal parameters are fixed in our simulations.

In the rest of the chapter, first we address temporal data representation issues, then motivation and the proposed approach is described, and then the proposed WCE algorithm is presented along with algorithm analysis. After this, simulation results on a variety of temporal data clustering tasks are reported. At the end of the chapter we discuss issues relevant to our approach and draws conclusions.

7.2 WEIGHTED CLUSTERING ENSEMBLE WITH DIFFERENT REPRESENTATIONS OF TEMPORAL DATA

In this work, we propose a weighted consensus function guided by clustering validation criteria to reconcile initial partitions to candidate consensus partitions from different perspectives and then introduce an agreement function to further reconcile those candidate consensus partitions to a final partition. As a result, the proposed WCE algorithm provides an effective enabling technique for the joint use of different representations, which cuts the information loss in a single representation and exploits various information sources underlying temporal data. In addition, our approach tends to capture the intrinsic structure of a data set, for example, the number of clusters.

In this section, we first describe the motivation to propose our temporal data clustering model. Then, we present such model working on different representations via clustering ensemble learning.

7.2.1 MOTIVATION

It is known that different representations encode various structural information facets of temporal data in their representation space. For illustration, we perform the principal component analysis (PCA) on four typical representations described in Section 2.2.2 of a synthetic time series data set. The data set is produced by the stochastic function $F(t) = A \sin(2\pi\alpha t + B) + \varepsilon(t)$, where A, B, and α are free parameters and $\varepsilon(t)$ is the added noise drawn from the normal distribution N(0,1). The use of four different parameter sets (A, B, α) leads to time series of four classes and 100 time series in each class.

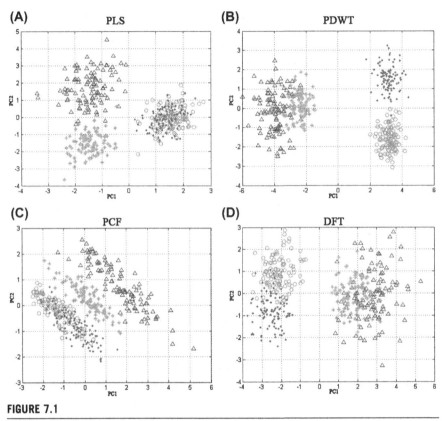

FIGURE 7.1

Distributions of the time series dataset in various principal component analysis representation manifolds formed by the first two principal components of their representations (Yang and Chen, 2011a). (A) PLS (B) PDWT (C) PCF (D) DFT.

Fig. 7.1 shows four representations of time series with various distributions in their PCA representation subspaces. Classes marked with blue triangles and magenta stars easily separate from the other two overlapped classes in Fig. 7.1A, while the same is true for the classes marked by green circles and red dots in Fig. 7.1B. Moreover, we can also gain such structural information from plots in Fig. 7.1C and D. Intuitively, our observation suggests that a single representation simply captures partial structural information, and the joint use of different representations is more likely to capture the intrinsic structure of a given temporal data set. When a clustering algorithm is applied to different representations, diverse partitions would be generated. To exploit all information sources, we need to reconcile diverse partitions to find out a consensus partition superior to any input partitions.

From Fig. 7.1, we also observe that the unlikelihood that partitions yielded by a clustering algorithm will carry an equal amount of useful information, due to their distributions in different representation spaces. The fact that most extant clustering ensemble methods treat all partitions equally during the reconciliation process, merely brings about an averaging effect. Based on our previous work (Yang, 2006; Yang and Chen, 2006), we have discovered various adverse outcomes in this area: clustering ensemble methods often yield a worse final partition, when the partitions to be combined are radically different. Moreover, the averaging effect is particularly harmful in a majority voting mechanism, especially as many highly correlated partitions appear inconsistent with the intrinsic structure of a given data set. All of this supports our belief in applying a different treatment to the input partitions: the measurement of their contributions with a weighted consensus function.

Without the ground truth, the contribution of a partition is actually unknown in general. Fortunately, existing clustering validation criteria (Halkidi et al., 2001) measure the clustering quality of a partition from different perspectives, for example, the validation of intraclass and interclass variation of clusters. To a great extent, we can employ clustering validation criteria to estimate contributions of partitions in terms of clustering quality. However, a clustering validation criterion often measures the clustering quality from a specific viewpoint only by simply highlighting a certain aspect. In order to estimate the contribution of a partition precisely in terms of clustering quality, we need to use various clustering validation criteria jointly. This idea is empirically justified by a simple example in the following section. In the following description, we omit technical details of WCEs, which will be presented in Section 7.2.3, for illustration only.

Fig. 7.2A shows a two-dimensional synthetic data set subject to a mixture of Gaussian distribution where there are five intrinsic clusters of heterogeneous structures, and the ground-truth partition is given for evaluation and marked by red (cluster 1), blue (cluster 2), black (cluster 3), cyan (cluster 4), and green (cluster 5). The visual inspection on the structure of the data set shown in Fig. 7.2A suggests that clusters 1 and 2 are relatively separate while cluster 3 spreads widely, and clusters 4 and 5 of different populations overlap each other.

Applying the K-means algorithm on different initialization conditions, including the center of clusters and the number of clusters, to the data set yields 20 partitions. Using different clustering validation criteria (Halkidi et al., 2001), we evaluate the clustering quality of each single partition. Fig. 7.2B−D depict single partitions of maximum value in terms of different criteria. The Dunn's Validity Index (DVI) criterion always favors a partition of balanced structure. Although the partition in Fig. 7.2B meets this criterion well, it properly groups clusters 1−3 only but fails to work on clusters 4 and 5. The Modified Huber's Γ index (MHΓ) criterion generally favors partition with bigger number of clusters. The partition in Fig. 7.2C meets this criterion but fails to group clusters 1−3 properly. Similarly, the partition in Fig. 7.2D fails to separate clusters 4 and 5 but is still judged as the best partition in terms of the Normalized Mutual Information (NMI) criterion that favors the most common structures detected in all partition.

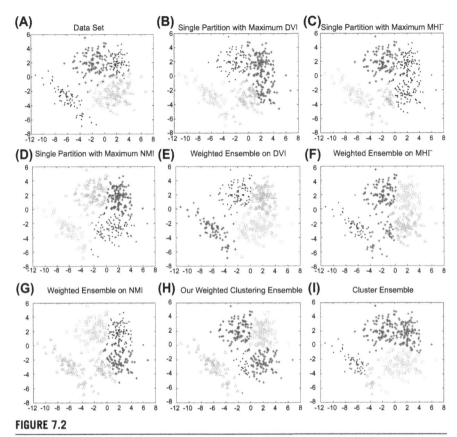

FIGURE 7.2

Results of clustering analysis and clustering ensembles (Yang and Chen, 2011a). (A) The data set of ground truth. (B) The partition of maximum DVI. (C) The partition of maximum MHΓ. (D) The partition of maximum NMI. (E) DVI WCE. (F) MHΓ WCE. (G) NMI WCE. (H) Multiple criteria WCE. (I) The Cluster Ensemble (Strehl and Ghosh 2003). *DVI*, Dunn's Validity Index; *MHΓ*, Modified Huber's Γ index; *NMI*, Normalized Mutual Information; *WCE*, weighted clustering ensemble.

By the use of a single criterion to estimate the contribution of partitions in the WCE, it inevitably leads to incorrect consensus partitions as illustrated in Fig. 7.2E–G, respectively. As three criteria reflect different yet complementary facets of clustering quality, the joint use of them to estimate the contribution of partitions become a natural choice. As illustrated in Fig. 7.2H, the consensus partition yielded by the multiple criteria–based WCE is very close to the ground truth in Fig. 7.2A. As a classic approach, cluster ensemble (CE) (Strehl and Ghosh, 2003) treats all partitions equally during reconciling input partitions. When applied to this data set, it yields a consensus partition shown in Fig. 7.2I that fails to detect the intrinsic structure underlying the data set.

In summary, the previous intuitive demonstration strongly suggests the joint use of different representations for temporal data clustering and the necessity of developing a WCE algorithm.

7.2.2 MODEL DESCRIPTION

Thus motivated, we propose a temporal data clustering model with a WCE working on different representations. As illustrated in Fig. 7.3, the model consists of three modules, that is, feature extraction, initial clustering analysis, and WCE.

1. In the representation extraction module, different representations are extracted by transforming raw temporal data to feature vectors of fixed dimensionality for initial clustering analysis. Because various representations of a complementary nature are demanded in our ensemble model, we recommend the use of both piecewise and global temporal data representations. Therefore, four representations presented in Section 2.2.2 would be applied in the simulation.
2. In the initial clustering analysis module, a clustering algorithm is applied to different representations received from the representation extraction module. As a result, a partition for a given data set is generated based on each representation. When a clustering algorithm of different parameters is used, for example, K-means, more partitions based on a representation would be produced by

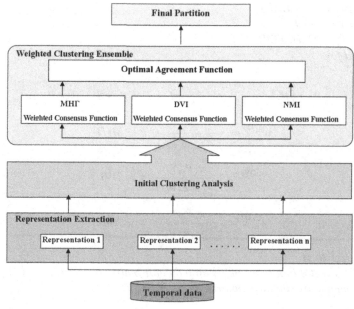

FIGURE 7.3

WCE with different representations (Yang and Chen, 2011a).

running the algorithm on various initialization conditions. Thus, the clustering analysis on different representations leads to multiple partitions for a given data set. All partitions achieved will be fed to the WCE module for the reconciliation to a final partition.

3. In the WCE module, a weighted consensus function works on three clustering validation criteria to estimate the contribution of each partition received from the initial clustering analysis module. The consensus function with single criterion−based weighting schemes yields three candidate consensus partitions, respectively, as presented in Section 7.2.3. Then, candidate consensus partitions are fed to the agreement function presented in Section 7.2.4, to form a final agreed partition where the number of clusters is automatically determined.

A pseudo code is also provided in the following section.
Input:

- *a data set $X = \{x1, x2,..., xN\}$.*
- *an integer R (number of feature representations)*
- *an integer T (number of iterations)*
- *the feature extraction function FEATURE*
- *the clustering algorithm, CLUSTERING*
- *Clustering validity index π*
- *DSPA consensus function, DSPA*

> *for r = 1 to R.*
>   *fr = FEATURE$_r$(X)*
>   *for t = 1 to T.*
>   *$P^r_t = CLUSTERING(f_r)$;*
>   *end for*
> *end for*

$$P = \left\{P^r_t\right\}_{t=1,...,T;\ r=1,...,R}; \ M = T \times R \rightarrow |P|; \ P_m \in P,$$

$$w^{MHT}_m = \frac{\pi(P_m)}{\sum^M_{m=1}\pi(P_m)}, \ \pi = MHT$$

$$w^{DVI}_m = \frac{\pi(P_m)}{\sum^M_{m=1}\pi(P_m)}, \ \pi = DVI$$

$$w^{NMI}_m = \frac{\pi(P_m)}{\sum^M_{m=1}\pi(P_m)}, \ \pi = NMI$$

> *for m = 1 to M.*
>   *Construct a binary membership indicator matrix of P_m: $H_m = \{0,1\}^{N \times K_m}$*
>   *Compute its similarity matrix: $S_m = H_m H^{Tr}_m$*
> *end for*

$$S^{MHT} = \sum_{m=1}^{M} w_m^{MHT} S_m; \ S^{DVI} = \sum_{m=1}^{M} w_m^{DVI} S_m; \ S^{NMI} = \sum_{m=1}^{M} w_m^{NMI} S_m;$$

$$P^{MHT} = DSPA\left(S^{MHT}\right); \ P^{DVI} = DSPA\left(S^{DVI}\right); \ P^{NMI} = DSPA\left(S^{NMI}\right);$$

Construct a binary membership indicator matrix $H = \left[H^{MHT}|H^{DVI}|H^{NMI}\right]$ based on consensus partitions. $\{P^{MHT}, P^{DVI}, P^{NMI}\}$
Compute the similarity matrix: $\overline{S} = \frac{1}{3} H H^{Tr}$

$$\overline{P} = DSPA\left(\overline{S}\right)$$

Output: the final partition $\overline{P}$.

7.2.3 WEIGHTED CONSENSUS FUNCTION

Weighted consensus function lies the essential idea of using the pairwise similarity between objects in a partition for evident accumulation. In this approach, a pairwise similarity matrix is derived from weighted partitions and weights are determined by measuring the clustering quality with different clustering validation criteria, then, a dendrogram (Jain et al., 1999) is constructed based on all similarity matrices to generate candidate consensus partitions.

Partition Weighting Scheme

Assume that $X = \{\mathbf{x}_n\}_{n=1}^{N}$ is a data set of N objects and there are M partitions $P = \{P_m\}_{m=1}^{M}$ on X, where the cluster number in M partitions could be different, as obtained by initial clustering analysis. Our partition weighting scheme assigns a weight w_m^{π} to each P_m in terms of a clustering validation criterion π, and weights for all partitions based on the criterion π collectively form a weight vector $\mathbf{w}^{\pi} = \{w_m^{\pi}\}_{m=1}^{M}$ for the partition collection P. In the partition weighting scheme, we define a weight

$$w_m^{\pi} = \frac{\pi(P_m)}{\sum_{m=1}^{M} \pi(P_m)}, \tag{7.1}$$

where $w_m^{\pi} > 0$ and $\sum_{m=1}^{M} w_m^{\pi} = 1$. $\pi(P_m)$ is the clustering validity index value in terms of the criterion π. Intuitively, the weight of a partition would express its contribution to the combination in terms of its clustering quality measured by the clustering validation criterion π.

In order to estimate the contribution of a partition, we examine as many different aspects of clustering quality as possible. After looking into all existing of clustering validation criteria, we select three criteria of complementary nature for generating weights from different perspectives, that is, MHΓ, DVI, and NMI. As has already been mentioned in Section 3.3, these criteria each measure only an aspect of clustering quality and all behave differently. For instance, MHΓ strongly favors a partition with more clusters. As with MHΓ, the DVI is insensitive to the number of clusters in a partition but is significantly less robust due to its use of a single linkage distance and the diameter information of clusters. As a result, it is quite sensitive to noise or outliers for any cluster of a large diameter. Intuitively, a high NMI value suggests a well-accepted partition that is more likely to reflect the intrinsic structure of a given data set. This criterion shows bias toward the highly correlated partitions and favors clusters containing a similar number of objects.

Finally three weight vectors, $\mathbf{w}^{MHT}$, $\mathbf{w}^{DVI}$, and $\mathbf{w}^{NMI}$ are obtained by respectively substituting π for a specific clustering validity index and are then used to weigh the similarity matrix, respectively.

Weighted Similarity Matrix

For each partition P_m, a binary membership indicator matrix $H_m = \{0, 1\}^{N \times K_m}$ is constructed where K_m is the number of clusters in the partition P_m. In the matrix H_m, a row corresponds to one datum and a column refers to a binary encoding vector for one specific cluster in the partition P_m. Entities of the column with one indicates that the corresponding objects are grouped into the same cluster and zero otherwise. Now we can use the matrix H_m to derive an $N \times N$ binary similarity matrix S_m which encodes the pairwise similarity between any two objects in a partition. For each partition P_m, its similarity matrix $S_m = \{0, 1\}^{N \times N}$ is constructed by

$$S_m = H_m H_m^{Tr} \tag{7.2}$$

In Eq. (7.2), the element $(S_m)_{ij}$ is equal to the inner product between rows i and j of the matrix H_m. Therefore, objects i and j are grouped into the same cluster if the element $(S_m)_{ij} = 1$ and in different clusters otherwise.

Finally, a weighted similarity matrix S^π concerning all the partitions in P is constructed from a linear combination of their similarity matrix S_m and their weight w_m^π as

$$S^\pi = \sum_{m=1}^{M} w_m^\pi S_m. \tag{7.3}$$

In this approach, three weighted similarity matrices, S^{MHT}, S^{DVI}, and S^{NMI} are constructed, respectively.

Candidate Consensus Partition Generation

A weighted similarity matrix S^π is used to reflect the collective relationship between all data in terms of different partitions and a clustering validation criterion π. However, the weighted similarity matrix actually tends to accumulate evidence in terms of clustering quality and hence treats all partitions differently.

Motivated by the technique used by Fred and Jain (2005), we employ the dendrogram-based similarity partitioning algorithm (DSPA) developed in our previous work (Yang and Chen, 2007) to produce a candidate consensus partition from a weighted similarity matrix S^π. DSPA algorithm makes use of an average-link hierarchical clustering (HC) algorithm. This converts the weighted similarity matrix into a dendrogram (Jain et al., 1999) with all the data in a given data set indexed in its horizontal axis and the lifetime of all possible cluster formations expressed in the vertical.

The lifetime of a cluster in the dendrogram is defined as an interval from the moment that this cluster is created to the moment that it disappears by merging with other clusters. Here, we would emphasize that, due to the use of a weighted similarity matrix, the lifetime of clusters is weighted by clustering quality in terms of a specific clustering validation criterion. Therefore, the dendrogram will differ from that yielded by a similarity matrix without a weighting component (Fred and Jain, 2005).

Consequently, the number of clusters in the candidate consensus partition P^π can be determined automatically by cutting the dendrogram derived from S^π to form clusters at the longest lifetime. Using the DSPA algorithm, we achieve three candidate consensus partitions P^π, $\pi = \{\text{MH}\Gamma, \text{DVI}, \text{NMI}\}$, in this approach.

7.2.4 AGREEMENT FUNCTION

The proposed weighted consensus function yields three candidate consensus partitions, respectively, according to three different clustering validation criteria. In general, these partitions are not always consistent with each other (see Fig. 7.2 for example), and hence, a further reconciliation is required for a final partition as the output of the proposed clustering ensemble model.

In order to obtain a final partition, we develop an agreement function by means of the evident accumulation (Fred and Jain, 2005) again. A pairwise similarity $\overline{S}$ is constructed with three candidate consensus partitions in the same way as described in Section 7.2.3. That is, a binary membership indicator matrix H^π is constructed from partition P^π where $\pi = \{\text{MH}\Gamma, \text{DVI}, \text{NMI}\}$. Then, concatenating three H^π matrices leads to an adjacency matrix consisting of all the data in a given data set versus candidate consensus partitions, $H = \left[H^{MH\Gamma} | H^{DVI} | H^{NMI} \right]$. Thus, the pairwise similarity matrix $\overline{S}$ is achieved by

$$\overline{S} = \frac{1}{3} H H^{Tr} \tag{7.4}$$

Finally, a dendrogram is derived from $\overline{S}$ and the final partition $\overline{P}$ is achieved by using DSPA algorithm.

7.2.5 ALGORITHM ANALYSIS

Under the assumption that any partition of a given data set is a noisy version of its ground-truth partition subject to the normal distribution (Topchy et al., 2004), the clustering ensemble problem can be viewed as finding a "mean" partition of input partitions in general. If we know the ground-truth partition, P_c, and all possible partitions, P_t, of the given data set, the ground-truth partition would be the "mean" of all possible partitions (Topchy et al., 2004):

$$P_C = \arg\min_P \sum_i \Pr(P_i = P_c) d(P_i, P), \tag{7.5}$$

where $\Pr(P_i = P_c)$ is the probability that P_c, is randomly distorted to be P_t and $d(\cdot, \cdot)$ is a distance metric for any two partitions. Under the normal distribution assumption, $\Pr(P_i = P_c)$ is proportional to the similarity between P_t and P_c.

In a practical clustering ensemble problem, an initial clustering analysis process returns only a partition subset, $\mathbf{P} = \{P_m\}_{m=1}^M$. From Eq. (7.5), finding the "mean", P^*, of M partitions in P can be performed by minimizing the cost function:

$$\Phi(P) = \sum_{m=1}^M \mu_m d(P_m, P), \tag{7.6}$$

where $\mu_m \propto \Pr(P_m = P_c)$ and $\sum_{m=1}^M \mu_m = 1$. The optimal solution to minimizing (7.6) is the intrinsic "mean", P^* :

$$P^* = \arg\min_P \sum_{m=1}^M \mu_m d(P_m, P). \tag{7.7}$$

In this work, we use the piecewise similarity matrix to characterize a partition and hence define the distance as $d(P_m, P) = \|S_m - S\|^2$ where S is the similarity matrix of a consensus partition, P. Thus, Eq. (7.6) can be rewritten as

$$\Phi(P) = \sum_{m=1}^M \mu_m \|S_m - S\|^2. \tag{7.8}$$

Let S^* be the similarity matrix of the "mean", P^*. Finding P^* to minimize $\Phi(P)$ in Eq. (7.8) is analytically solvable (Cox et al., 2006), that is, $S^* = \sum_{m=1}^M \mu_m S_m$. By connecting this optimal "mean" to the cost function in Eq. (7.8), we have

$$\begin{aligned}
\Phi(P) &= \sum_{m=1}^M \mu_m \|S_m - S\|^2 \\
&= \sum_{m=1}^M \mu_m \|(S_m - S^*) + (S^* - S)\|^2 \\
&= \sum_{m=1}^M \mu_m \|(S_m - S^*)\|^2 + \sum_{m=1}^M \mu_m \|(S^* - S)\|^2.
\end{aligned} \tag{7.9}$$

Note that the fact $\sum_{m=1}^M \mu_m \|S_m - S^*\| = 0$ is applied in the last step of Eq. (7.9) due to $\sum_{m=1}^M \mu_m = 1$ and $S^* = \sum_{m=1}^M \mu_m S_m$. The actual cost of a consensus partition is now decomposed into two terms in Eq. (7.9). The first term corresponds to the quality of input partitions, for example, how close they are to the ground-truth partition, P_c, solely determined by an initial clustering analysis regardless of clustering ensemble. In other words, the first term is constant once the initial clustering analysis returns a collection of partitions, P. The second term is determined by the performance of a clustering ensemble algorithm that yields the consensus partition, P, that is, how close the consensus partition is to the weighted "mean" partition. Thus, Eq. (7.9) provides a generic measure to analyze a clustering ensemble algorithm.

In our WCE algorithm, a consensus partition is an estimated "mean" characterized in a generic form: $S = \sum_{m=1}^M w_m S_m$, where w_m is w_m^π yielded by a single clustering validation criterion π, or $\bar{w}_m$ produced by the joint use of multiple criteria.

By inserting the estimated "mean" in the previously mentioned form and the intrinsic "mean" into Eq. (7.9), the second term of Eq. (7.9) becomes

$$\sum_{m=1}^{M} \mu_m \left\| \sum_{m=1}^{M} (\mu_m - w_m) S_m \right\|^2 . \tag{7.10}$$

From Eq. (7.10), it is observed that the quantities $|\mu_m - w_m|$ critically determine the performance of a WCE.

It has been assumed in clustering analysis that an underlying structure can be detected if it holds well-defined cluster properties, such as compactness, separability, and cluster stability (Jain et al., 1999; Halkidi et al., 2001; Xu and Wunsch, 2005). We expect that such properties to be measurable by clustering validation criteria so that w_m is as close to μ_m as possible. In reality, the ground-truth partition is generally not available for a given data set, and without the knowledge of μ_m, it is impossible to formally analyze how good any given clustering validation criteria are for estimating intrinsic weights. Instead, we undertake empirical studies to investigate its capacity and limitation of our WCE algorithm based on elaborately designed synthetic data sets of the ground-truth information, which is presented in Appendix.

7.3 SIMULATION

In this section, we present our experimental methodology and report simulation results. Despite the wide range of applications suitable to clustering analysis, we focus only on clustering-based classification tasks which organize objects into groups based on chosen similarity measures (Euclidean distance on time series benchmarks and CAVIAR database, correlation on Physiological Data Modeling Contest - PDMC time series data stream), with no labeling information on the target data set. In simulations, to examine the legitimacy of fundamental concepts associated with our approach, we apply our proposed WCE to several benchmark data sets for time series data mining (Keogh, 2003). An objective trajectory benchmark of the CAVIAR visual tracking database (CAVIAR, 2002) and a time series data stream of the PDMC sensor data set (PDMC, 2004) are used to evaluate the robustness and feasibility of the proposed approach.

7.3.1 TIME SERIES BENCHMARKS

Time series benchmarks of 16 synthetic or real-world time series data sets (Keogh, 2003) have been collected to evaluate a number of temporal data classification and clustering algorithms in the context of temporal data mining. In this collection, the ground truth, that is, the class label of time series in a data set, is available and each data set is further divided into the training and testing subsets in advance for the evaluation of a classification algorithm. This benchmarks has been also used for evaluating the previous proposed ensemble approaches presented in this book, the information on all 16 data sets is tabulated in 5.3, including the number of classes, the number of time series, and the length of time series in every data set.

Three sets of experiments are carried out in this simulation. First, we employ classic temporal-proximity and model-based approaches on this time series benchmark. There are Dynamic Time Warping-based K-means (DTW K-means), HC algorithm, and K-means-based HMM K-model clustering, the performance of the K-means algorithm is provided by benchmark collectors. Second, we examine clustering performance on four representations to see if the use of a single representation is sufficient for temporal data clustering. For this we employ two well-known algorithms, that is, K-means, an essential algorithm and, DBSCAN, a more sophisticated density-based algorithm that can discover clusters of arbitrary shape and offers good model selection ability. Third, we apply our WCE algorithm to combine the input partitions collectively yielded by K-means, HC, and DBSCAN with different representations during the initial clustering analysis.

For the first set of experiments, we directly apply DTW K-means, HC and HMM K-models under the same condition on the benchmarks, where allows both of DTW K-means and HMM K-model to use the correct cluster number, K^*, the results of K-means is provided by benchmark collector, and no parameter setting in HC. For second set of experiments, K^* is also pre-defined for K-means. Although DBSCAN requires no prior knowledge of a given data set, two parameters in the algorithm need to be tuned for the good performance (Ester et al., 1996). As suggested in the literature (Ester et al., 1996), we find the best parameters for each data set by an exhaustive search within a proper parameter range. Given the fact that K-means is sensitive to initial conditions even though K^* is given, we run the algorithm 10 times on each data set with different initial conditions in the two aforementioned experiments. The results are used for comparison to the clustering ensemble. Thus, only the best results are reported, in the interests of fairness.

For the third set of experiments, we use K-means as a base learner without prior knowledge, K*, to produce partitions on different representations, which is designed to test model-selection capability of the proposed ensemble model. As a result, we take the following procedure to produce a partition by K-means. With a random number generator of uniform distribution, we draw a number within the range $K^* - 2 \leq K \leq K^* + 2 (K > 0)$ used in K-means to produce a partition on an initial condition. For each data set, we repeat the previously mentioned procedure to produce 10 partitions on a single representation so that there are totally 40 partitions during initial clustering analysis. As mentioned previously, there is no parameter setting in the HC and, therefore, only one partition is yielded for a given data set. Thus, we need to combine only four partitions returned by the HC on four representations for each data set. When DBSCAN is used in initial clustering analysis on different representations, we combine four best partitions of each data set achieved from single-representation experiments mentioned previously. Here, we emphasize that there is no parameter tuning in our simulations. Internal parameters of the representations for all 16 data sets are fixed, and as used by the benchmark collectors (Keogh, 2003), the classification accuracy described in Section 3.3.1 is used to evaluate the performance of compared approaches.

Table 7.1 lists all results achieved in the three sets of experiments. The first part of results shows that DTW K-means outperforms K-means and HC, HMM K-model, on 11 of the 16 data sets. Given the fact of that HC is capable of finding a cluster number, we also report the model-selection performance of HC noting that * is added behind the classification accuracy if it finds the correct cluster number. As a result, HC manages to find the correct cluster number for four data sets only, indicating the challenges inherent in clustering temporal data of high dimensions. It is necessary to mention that the HMM K-model takes a considerably longer time to perform when compared with other algorithms, including the proposed clustering ensembles.

The second part of results also shows that, with regard to clustering performance on single representations, no one can always lead to best performance on all data sets, regardless of which algorithm is used or that the winning performance is achieved across four representations. The results simply demonstrate how difficult the choice of representation is. DBSCAN is generally better than K-means algorithm on the appropriate representation space. In total, it correctly detects the right cluster number for 9 of 16 data sets with appropriate representations and the best parameter setup. This implies the difficulties in model selection in the single representation space, in other words, a sophisticated algorithm does not perform well due to lost information at the representation extraction stage.

In terms of both classification accuracy and model selection, and regardless of the algorithm used in initial clustering analysis, the third part of the table shows the significantly enhanced performance of the proposed ensemble approach. In general, the ensemble result on different representations outperforms the best result yielded by the same algorithm on single representations, and even the average result achieved by the proposed ensemble model is better than the best result from single representations when K-means is used. In model selection, the proposed ensemble model fails to detect the right cluster number for only 2 and 1 of the 16 data sets only, respectively, with K-means and HC used in initial clustering analysis. While the proposed ensemble model with a base learner of DBSCAN is successful for detecting the correct number of clusters on 10 of the 16 data sets. The bold entries in Table 7.1 shows the best results achieved. It is observed that the proposed ensemble approach achieves the best classification accuracy for 12 of the 16 data sets, in which K-means, HC, and DBSCAN are used as base learner to achieve best performance for six, two, and four data sets, respectively.

For comparison, we further employ three state-of-the-art ensemble learning approach on the benchmarks, these approaches include: CE (Strehl and Ghosh, 2003), hybrid bipartite graph formulation (HBGF) algorithm (Fern and Brodley, 2004), and semi-definite programming–based clustering ensemble (SDP-CE) (Singh et al., 2007). This simulation uses K-means for initial clustering analysis. Due to the fact of that all three ensemble approaches were developed without reference to model-selection problems, we use the correct cluster number K^* for each data set. Therefore, 10 partitions are generated with different initial conditions on

Table 7.1 Classification Accuracy (%)[a] of Different Clustering Algorithms on Time Series Benchmarks

Data Set	Time Series				Single Representation								Different Representations		
					K-means				DBSCAN				WCE		
	K-means	DTW K-means	HC	HMM K-model	PCF	DFT	PLS	PDWT	PCF	DFT	PLS	PDWT	K-means	HC	DBSCAN
Syn control	67.9	69.8	59.5	69.1	58.3	62.4	64.7	68.5	34.5	70.0*	70.4*	55.8	86.1 ± 2.5*	73.8*	78.2*
Gun-point	50.0	65.6	41.9*	43.8	44.3	43.2	47.0	48.3	48.1*	51.5*	42.4	50.0*	54.1 ± 1.8*	69.1*	52.0*
CBF	62.6	80.9	50.9	60.1	53.5	49.3	52.9	61.2	53.8*	46.7	51.7	62.9*	63.9 ± 2.1*	70.7*	63.2*
Face (all)	36.0	49.4	31.9	37.8	31.5	30.2	32.1	33.4	13.6	34.7	19.9	32.3	51.9 ± 1.4*	50.2*	33.9
OSU leaf	37.8	35.1	39.1*	44.2	32.6	29.3	31.4	35.7	20.9	21.6	25.0	39.9*	45.5 ± 3.5*	45.9*	46.2*
Swedish leaf	40.6	48.1	35.6	38.6	34.3	33.5	36.9	38.1	14.4	25.3	32.7	32.9	59.8 ± 2.1*	56.4*	38.3*
50words	42.0	37.2	39.5	40.8	34.2	36.1	32.3	37.0	32.7	30.6	32.5	29.3	37.2 ± 2.7	46.9*	36.1
Trace	48.5	63.4	40.2	50.9	39.6	42.3	41.8	46.3	33.3	43.7	47.5	49.5	57.2 ± 2.3*	58.0	60.6*
Two patterns	32.2	56.3	29.8	33.1	26.1	27.6	29.2	32.0	24.7	27.4	21.9	21.3	37.7 ± 2.5*	38.3*	29.0
Wafer	62.5	47.5	53.2	63.9	55.3	59.8	54.8	61.8	71.9*	54.4*	59.1	38.4	71.7 ± 2.4*	69.7*	73.3*
Face (four)	66.9	70.7	62.7*	69.1	49.3	55.3	60.3	67.2	17.3	17.2	35.1	49.1	78.9 ± 3.0*	75.8*	51.7
Lightning-2	61.1	62.1	62.0*	57.7	52.1	53.5	54.3	56.1	62.4*	56.7	45.7	43.7	77.9 ± 1.8*	75.1*	71.9*
Lightning-7	48.4	50.5	39.4	51.2	40.7	42.6	48.3	49.2	44.0	33.7	45.7*	33.8	58.7 ± 3.4*	56.7*	53.9*
ECG	69.8	62.8	59.4	70.3	58.8	61.0	61.4	62.2	49.0*	50.6*	47.6*	60.9*	69.0 ± 1.7*	73.5*	74.9*
Adiac	38.4	39.6	30.2	38.9	30.9	29.3	32.1	31.6	32.0	12.6	33.1	25.3	36.8 ± 2.5	33.6	34.2
Yoga	51.7	56.3	44.2	48.5	59.1	52.6	46.8	51.0	46.1	66.8*	41.6	43.3	62.6 ± 2.0*	64.3*	67.5

HC, hierarchical clustering; HMM, hidden Markov model; WCE, weighted clustering ensemble.
[a] Notation of correct cluster number determined.

single representation, in turn, 40 partitions are totally obtained from four different representations. In our WCE, we use the same procedure described earlier for K-means to produce partitions, where K is randomly chosen from $K^* - 2 \leq K \leq K^* + 2(K > 0)$. We conduct 10 trials and report the average and standard deviations of classification accuracy rates.

Table 7.2 shows the performance of four clustering ensemble approaches using the same notation as in Table 7.1. It is observed that the SDP-CE, HBGF, and CE algorithms win on five, two, and one data sets, respectively, while the proposed WCE algorithm achieves best results for the remaining eight data sets. Closer observation indicates that for four of the eight data sets where other algorithms win, WCE algorithm achieves the second best results. SDP-CE suffers from the highest computational burden, while WCE incurs higher computational costs than the CE and the HBGF. Considering its capability of model selection and a trade-off between performance and computational efficiency, we believe that our WCE algorithm is especially suitable for temporal data clustering with different representations.

In order to make comparison between three proposed ensemble approaches including *HMM-based meta-clustering ensemble, Iteratively constructed clustering ensemble with a hybrid sampling, WCE with multiple representations* presented in this book, we further summarize the experimental results obtained by these three approaches on the time series benchmark. We employ K-means as base learner, where the K value as cluster number is selected from a preset range $K^* - 2 \leq K \leq K^* + 2(K > 0)$ for both of *HMM-based meta-clustering ensemble* and *WCE with multiple representations*, and the correct cluster number K^* is pre-defined for *Iteratively*

Table 7.2 Classification Accuracy (%)[a] of Clustering Ensembles on Time Series Benchmarks (Yang and Chen, 2011a)

Data Set	CE	HBGF	SDP-CE	WCE
Syn control	68.8 + 2.1	74.8 ± 2.2	82.1 + 1.9	**86.1 ± 2.5***
Gun-point	51.8 + 1.4	53.8 ± 2.0	50.0 ± 0.9	**54.1 ± 1.8***
CBF	53.8 + 2.4	66.0 ± 1.9	**66.3 ± 2.1**	63.9 ± 2.1*
Face (all)	35.1 + 1.9	44.8 ± 2.5	50.5 ± 1.2	**51.9 ± 1.4***
OSU leaf	35.2 + 1.7	**48.1 ± 2.9**	46.9 ± 2.1	45.5 ± 3.5*
Swedish leaf	41.2 + 0.8	52.8 ± 2.3	**62.6 ± 1.8**	59.8 ± 2.1*
50words	**39.6 + 1.6**	39.1 ± 2.1	38.9 ± 1.9	37.2 ± 2.7
Trace	50.5 + 2.0	**45.6 ± 2.2**	55.1 ± 1.9	**57.2 ± 2.3***
Two patterns	33.1 + 1.8	**33.0 ± 1.9**	36.9 ± 2.3	**37.7 ± 2.5***
Wafer	62.1 + 1.9	**72.8 ± 2.6**	70.0 ± 2.4	71.7 ± 24*
Face (four)	**65.2 + 2.1**	72.1 ± 3.1	71.8 ± 3.5	**78.9 ± 3.0***
Lightning-2	**60.1 + 1.3**	59.3 ± 2.1	66.2 ± 1.6	**77.9 ± 1.8***
Lightning-7	**53.1 + 2.1**	55.6 ± 3.0	57.9 ± 2.4	**58.7 ± 3.4***
ECG	65.2 + 1.6	68.7 ± 2.0	**69.2 ± 1.7**	69.0 ± 1.7*
Adiac	36.2 + 2.3	41.4 ± 2.5	**45.9 ± 1.9**	36.8 ± 2.5
Yoga	50.6 + 2.3	60.0 ± 2.2	**68.2 ± 2.2**	62.6 ± 2.0 *

CE, cluster ensemble; *HBGF*, hybrid bipartite graph formulation; *SDP-CE*, semi-definite programming—based clustering ensemble; *WCE*, weighted clustering ensemble.
[a] Notation of correct cluster number determined.

constructed clustering ensemble with a hybrid sampling during their initial clustering analysis due to their own model-selection abilities. Following exactly same experimental setup described previously, we run this simulation 10 times with best parameter setup, and the best results obtained by three proposed ensemble approaches are reported in Table 7.3. As shown in this table, *WCE with multiple representations* has the best performance on 9 out of 16 data sets. *HMM-based meta-clustering ensemble* achieves best results for five data sets, *Iteratively constructed clustering ensemble with a hybrid sampling* win on two. Given the fact that both of *HMM-based meta-clustering ensemble* and *WCE with multiple representations* are capable for finding a cluster number in a given data set by using DSPA consensus function, we also report their model selection performance with the former notation (*). As a result, *WCE with multiple representations* once again achieves the best results that is able to find the correct cluster number on 14 out of 16 data sets, and *HMM-based meta clustering ensemble* also manages to find the correct cluster number for 11 data sets.

To conclude, in comparison with classical temporal data clustering, "state-of-the-art" clustering ensemble algorithms, and even two former proposed ensemble approaches, the favorable results achieved on the benchmark time series collection

Table 7.3 Classification Accuracy (%)[a] of Our Proposed Clustering Ensemble Models on Time Series Benchmarks

Data Set	HMM Hybrid Meta-Ensemble Clustering	Iteratively Constructed Clustering Ensemble With Hybrid Sampling	Weighted Clustering Ensemble With Multiple Representations
Syn control	73.2*	74.3	**88.6***
Gun-point	**65.2***	56.7	55.9*
CBF	64.3*	64.8	**66.0***
Face (all)	31.4	40.4	**53.3***
OSU leaf	38.0	41.8	**49.0***
Swedish leaf	42.5*	44.6	**61.9***
50words	**46.2***	40.9	39.9
Trace	**63.9***	53.5	59.5*
Two patterns	**50.6***	33.2	40.2*
Wafer	53.4	62.5	**74.1***
Face (four)	58.8	64.0	**81.9***
Lightning-2	67.6*	68.6	**79.7***
Lightning-7	50.0*	50.0	**62.1***
ECG	65.8	**72.0**	70.7*
Adiac	43.2*	**44.4**	39.3
Yoga	**63.8***	51.9	63.6*

HMM, hidden Markov model.
[a] *Notation of correct cluster number determined.*

clearly suggest the strengths and ease of use that our *WCE with multiple represen-tations* provides in temporal data clustering task.

7.3.2 MOTION TRAJECTORY

To explore potential applications, the proposed WCE is also applied on the CAVIAR database for trajectory clustering analysis, previously used in Chapters 5 and 6 for evaluating both of *HMM-based meta-clustering ensemble* and *Iteratively constructed clustering ensemble model*. Note that the preprocessing described in Section 6.3.3 is also required to normalize the trajectories into uniform length before feature extraction is applied to the trajectory dataset.

Given no prior knowledge of the "right" number of clusters for this database, K-means algorithm as the base learner is run 10 times by randomly choosing a K value from an interval between 5 and 25. 10 partitions are then generated with different initial conditions on each of four feature representations. In turn, total of 40 partitions are then fed to the proposed WCE to achieve the final partition shown in Fig. 7.4. Without the ground truth, we must apply human visual observa-tion for evaluating the results, as suggested by Khalid and Naftel (2005). In the language of common human visual experience, the behavior of pedestrians across the shopping mall can be roughly divided into five categories of motion behaviors: "move up," "move down," "stop," "move left," and "move right" (CAVIAR, 2002). Using clustering analysis, these behavioral trajectories are grouped together along a motion direction and used to infer and name different activities at a semantic level, for example, "enter the store," "exit from the store," "pass in front," and "stop to watch."

In Fig. 7.4, coherent motion trajectories have been properly grouped together while dissimilar ones are distributed into different clusters. For example, the trajec-tories corresponding to the activity of "stop to watch" are grouped accurately in the cluster shown in Fig. 7.4E. Those corresponding to "moving from left-to-right" or "right-to-left" are properly grouped into two separate clusters, shown in Fig. 7.4C and F. The trajectories "move up" and "move down" are grouped very effectively into the two clusters shown in Fig. 7.4J and K. Fig. 7.4A,D,G−I,N,O also indicate that trajectories corresponding to the activities "enter the store" and "exit the store" are properly grouped together via multiple clusters in light of various starting posi-tions, locations, motion direction, and so on. Finally, Fig. 7.4L and M illustrate two clusters roughly corresponding to the activity "pass in front."

As described in the Chapters 5 and 6, we have also examined former proposed approaches, which are *HMM-based meta-clustering ensemble* and *Iteratively con-structed clustering ensemble with a hybrid sampling*, on the CAVIAR database. Based on experimental results obtained by these proposed ensemble models, it is obvious that *HMM-based meta clustering ensemble* is quite different from other proposed ensemble models due to its insensitive to distinguish the trajectories following a similar motion path with opposite directions. For example, the trajec-tories corresponding to "move left" and "move right" trajectories shown in

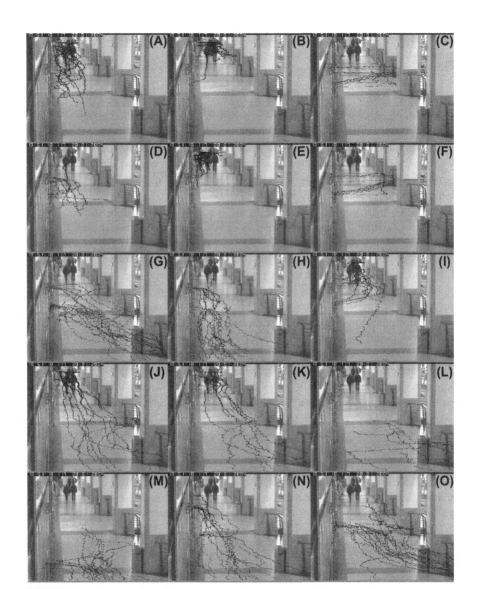

FIGURE 7.4

The final partition on the CAVIAR database by WCE with different representations; plots in (A)–(O) correspond to 15 clusters of moving trajectories (Yang and Chen, 2011a).

Fig. 6.6D and J obtained from *Iteratively constructed clustering ensemble with a hybrid sampling* or Fig. 7.4C and F obtained from *WCE with multiple representations* are grouped into a single cluster of "move vertically" shown in Fig. 5.8C obtained from *HMM-based meta-clustering ensemble*, while "move up" and "move down" trajectories shown in Fig. 6.6C and G obtained from *Iteratively constructed clustering ensemble with a hybrid sampling* or Fig. 7.4J,K and N obtained from *WCE with multiple representations* are either wholly or partially grouped into a cluster of "move vertically" shown in Fig. 5.8A. However, *HMM-based meta-clustering ensemble* is quite good at properly grouping the trajectories following the similar motion paths. For example, the trajectories corresponding to "enter store" shown in Fig. 5.8E obtained from *HMM-based meta-clustering ensemble* are separated into different clusters either shown in Fig. 6.6C and N obtained from *Iteratively constructed clustering ensemble with a hybrid sampling* or Fig. 7.4H and N obtained from *WCE with multiple representations*. On the other hand, we could identify that most of the clusters obtained from both of *Iteratively constructed clustering ensemble with a hybrid sampling* and *WCE with multiple representations*, respectively, are quite similar, and all trajectories are properly grouped into different clusters based on the similar motion behaviors, and these consistent and quality clustering results further justify the feasibility of fundamental concepts from different perspective. However, both algorithms still yield slightly different clustering results due to their own characteristics inherent in the different approaches. For *Iteratively constructed clustering ensemble with a hybrid sampling*, it significantly reduces the sensitivity to the noise data by using a subsampling schema. As illustrated in Fig. 6.6, a group of abnormal motion trajectories (noise data) shown in Fig. 6.6M are well separated from their closed "meaningful" motion trajectories shown in Fig. 6.6F. However, it improperly merges two groups of trajectories shown in Fig. 7.4H and J based on two different motion behaviors into single cluster shown in Fig. 6.6C due to similarity with the limited information in spatial domain. In contrast, *WCE with different representations*, which is presented in this chapter, is able to explore the hidden information exited in temporal data from different domains. As a result, the trajectories shown in Fig. 6.6C are well separated into two clusters shown in Fig. 7.4H and J, which is able to explore the detailed motion behaviors on the target data set. However, it fails to identify the abnormal motion trajectories in the cluster shown in Fig. 7.4O due to sensitive to the noise data. As a result, we believe that all proposed ensemble models behave differently with their own strength and weakness.

Moreover, we also record the execution time (117.98s) of *WCE with multiple representations* on CAVIAR database, which has been also applied for both of former proposed ensemble models presented in Chapters 5 and 6. By summering the implementation efficiency of three proposed ensemble models, where K is the number of clusters, N is the size of data set/number of objects, T is the number of ensemble members/input partitions, Table 7.4 shows that *Iteratively constructed clustering ensemble* has less computational complexity in comparison with others but it requires several key user—input parameters such as cluster number K. Although both of *HMM-*

Table 7.4 Computational Complexity of Our Proposed Clustering Ensemble Models on CAVIAR Database

Our Proposed Clustering Ensemble Models	Computational Complexity	Execution Time on the CAVIAR Database (s)
HMM based hybrid nieta-clustering ensemble	$\begin{cases} O(KN^2T) - CSPA \\ O(KNT) - HGPA \\ O(K^2NT^2) - MCLA \\ O(KN^2T) - DSPA \end{cases}$	4623.44
Iteratively constructed clustering ensemble with a hybrid sampling	$O(K3)$	12.27
Weighted clustering ensemble with multiple representations	$O(KN2T)$	117.98

HMM, *hidden Markov model.*

based meta-clustering ensemble and *WCE with multiple representations* demand higher computational resource, it requires minimum user-input parameters with automatic model-selection ability vice versa. Therefore, we believe that all proposed ensemble model behave differently with their own strength and weakness in terms of performance and computational cost.

The CAVIAR database was also used in the study by Khalid and Naftel (2005) where the self-organizing map with the single Discrete Fourier Transform representation was used for clustering analysis. In their simulation, the number of clusters was determined manually, and all trajectories were simply grouped into nine clusters. Although most clusters achieved in their simulation are consistent with ours, their method failed to separate a number of trajectories corresponding to different activities by simply putting them together into a cluster called "abnormal behaviors" instead. In contrast, ours properly groups them into several clusters shown in Fig. 7.4A,B,E and I. If the clustering analysis results are employed for modeling events or activities, their merged cluster inevitably fails to provide any useful information for a higher level analysis.

Clearly implying the benefits of the joint use of different representations, Fig. 7.5 illustrates several meaningless clusters of trajectories, judged by visual inspection, yielded by the same proposed approach but on single representations, respectively. Fig. 7.5A and B show that the sole use of a Polynomial Curve Fitting representation will create improper grouping of some trajectories of line structures along the x- and y-axes. The x and y components of these trajectories perpendicular to each other have a considerable coefficient value on their linear basis but only a tiny coefficient value on any higher order basis. Consequently, this leads to a short distance between such trajectories in the PCF representation space, which is responsible for improper grouping. Fig. 7.5C and D illustrate a limitation of the DFT representation, that is,

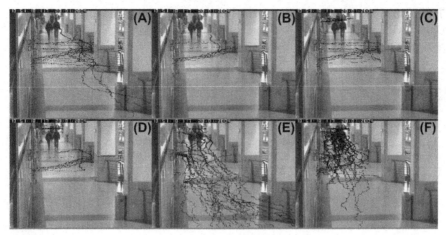

FIGURE 7.5

Meaningless clusters of trajectories on the CAVIAR database with a single representation.

trajectories with the same orientation but with different starting points are improperly grouped together since the DFT representation is in the frequency domain and therefore independent of spatial locations. Although the Piecewise Local Statistics and Piecewise Discrete Wavelet Transform representations highlight local features, global characteristics of trajectories could be neglected. The cluster based on the PLS representation shown in Fig. 7.5E improperly groups trajectories belonging to two clusters in Fig. 7.4K and N. Likewise, Fig. 7.5F shows an improper grouping based on the PDWT representation that merges three clusters in Fig. 7.4A,D and I. All the above results suggest that the joint use of different representations is capable of overcoming limitations of individual representations.

Two additional simulations take our evaluation further. The first tests the generalized performance on noisy data produced by adding different amount of Gaussian noise $N(0, \sigma)$ to the range of coordinates of the moving trajectories. The second simulates a scenario in which a tracked moving object is obstructed by other objects or by the background, leading inevitably to missing data in a trajectory. Fifty independent trials have been performed in our simulations, in the interests of securing a robust result.

Table 7.5 presents results of classifying noisy trajectories with the final partition shown in Fig. 7.4 where a decision is made by finding a cluster whose center is closest to the tested trajectory in terms of the Euclidean distance to see if its clean version belongs to this cluster. Apparently, the classification accuracy highly depends on the quality of clustering analysis. It is evident from Table 7.1 that the performance is satisfactory in contrast to those of the clustering ensemble on a single representation especially as a substantial amount of noise is added, which again demonstrates the synergy between different representations.

Table 7.5 Performance on the CAVIAR Corrupted With Noise (Yang and Chen, 2011a)

| Representation | WCE | | | |
	$\sigma = 0.1$	$\sigma = 0.2$	$\sigma = 0.3$	$\sigma = 0.4$
PCF	87.6 ± 2.6	81.7 ± 3.3	78.1 ± 3.7	72.9 ± 4.2
DFT	92.0 + 3.1	88.6 ± 3.5	85.9 ± 3.9	79.1 ± 3.6
PLS	95.2 ± 1.8	90.0 ± 2.5	89.5 ± 3.1	84.1 ± 4.0
PDWT	94.3 ± 2.8	90.1 ± 3.2	86.6 ± 2.6	84.2 ± 3.6
Multiple	**97.2 ± 1.7**	**93.1 ± 2.3**	**91.9 ± 1.9**	**85.9 ± 2.3**

WCE, *Weighted Clustering Ensemble.*

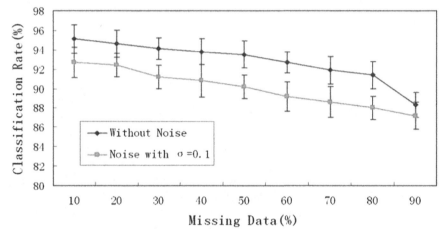

FIGURE 7.6

Classification accuracy of our WCE on the CAVIAR database and its noisy version in simulated occlusion situations.

To simulate missing data trajectories, we remove five identical segments of trajectory at random locations, while missing segments of various lengths are used for testing. We classify a trajectory of missing data using its observed data only. The same decision-making rule mentioned previously is also used. This simulation is conducted on all corrupted trajectories and their corresponding noisy versions by adding the Gaussian noise N(0, 0.1). Fig. 7.6 shows performance evolution in the presence of missing data measured by a percentage of the trajectory length. Our approach evidently performs well in simulated occlusion situations.

7.3.3 TIME-SERIES DATA STREAM

In contrast to temporal data collected prior to processing, a data stream consisting of variables comes from the continuous data flow of a given source, for example, sensor networks (PDMC, 2004), with high speeds generating examples over time. Hence, to perform clustering on a temporal data stream is to find groups of variables that behave similarly over time. Here, traditional temporal clustering algorithms meet with fresh challenges—an algorithm for temporal data stream clustering needs to effectively deal with each example in constant time and memory (Rodrigues et al., 2008).

Recent research with time-series data stream clustering algorithms, for example, the Online Divisive-Agglomerative Clustering (ODAC) algorithm (Rodrigues et al., 2008), has resulted in most such algorithms being developed to work on a stream fragment, thereby fulfilling clustering in constant time and memory. However, to fully exploit potential yet hidden information and to demonstrate the proposed approach in temporal data stream clustering, we also use the dynamic properties of a temporal data stream itself. It is known that dynamic properties of time series, $x(t)$, can be well described by its derivatives of different orders, $x^{(n)}(t), n = 1, 2, \ldots$ As a result, we would treat the derivatives of a stream fragment itself as different representations and then use them for the initial clustering analysis in our approach. Given that the estimate of the nth derivative requires only $n + 1$ successive points, a slightly larger constant memory is used in our approach that is, for the nth-order derivative of time series, the size of our memory is n points larger than the size of the memory used by the ODAC algorithm (Rodrigues et al., 2008).

Our simulations use the PDMC data set, collected from streaming sensor data of approximately 10,000 h of time-series data streams, containing several variables such as user ID, session ID, session time, two characteristics, annotation, gender, and nine sensors (PDMC, 2004). Following the same experimental setting as (Rodrigues et al., 2008), we use their ODAC algorithm for initial clustering analysis on three representations—time series, $x(t)$, and its first- and second-order derivatives, $x^{(1)}(t)$, and $x^{(2)}(t)$. We adopt the same criteria, MHΓ and DVI, used by (Rodrigues et al., 2008) to evaluate performance. This allows us a straightforward comparison between the proposed approach and this state-of-the-art technique,

Table 7.6 Results of the ODAC Algorithm Versus Our WCE (Yang and Chen, 2011a)

Data Set	ODAC			WCE		
	K	MHΓ	*DVI*	*K*	MHΓ	*DVI*
User ID = 6	3	0.377	0.891	5	0.418	1.931
User ID = 25	3	0.191	1.026	4	0.420	1.701

DVI, *Dunn's Validity Index; MHΓ, modified Huber's Γ index; ODAC, Online Divisive-Agglomerative Clustering; WCE, Weighted Clustering Ensemble.*

(A) Results (userID=6) generated by batch hierarchical clustering

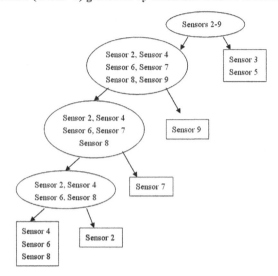

Results (userID=6) generated by our approach

(B) Results (userID=25) generated by batch hierarchical clustering

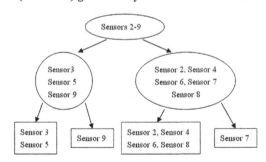

Results (userID=25) generated by our approach

FIGURE 7.7

Results of the batch hierarchical clustering algorithm versus our WCE on two data stream collections (Yang and Chen, 2011a). (A) User ID = 6; (B) user ID = 25.

and demonstrating the performance gain by the proposed ensemble approach via the exploitation of hidden yet potential information.

Table 7.6 displays the comparative results obtained by the proposed approach and those reported by (Rodrigues et al., 2008) on two collections: user ID = 6 of 80,182 observations and user ID = 25 of 141,251 observations. The task involved finding the correct number of clusters on eight sensors from 2 to 9. The best results on two collections are reported in the study Rodrigues et al. (2008). Working on the time-series data streams, their ODAC algorithm only finds three sensor clusters for each user. Their clustering quality is evaluated by the MHΓ and the DVI. Table 7.6 shows our approach to achieve much higher MHΓ and DVI values while finding considerably different cluster structures, there are five clusters found for user ID = 6 and four clusters found for user ID = 25.

Despite outperforming the ODAC algorithm in terms of clustering quality criteria, we still would not conclude that our approach is much better than the ODAC algorithm as those criteria evaluate clustering quality from a specific perspective only. Although there is no ground truth available we believe that a whole stream of all observations should contain precise information on its intrinsic structure and be able to verify our results by comparing it with the result obtained by a batch hierarchical clustering (BHC) algorithm (Johnson, 1967). Fig. 7.7 shows the resultant similarities and contrasts between the BHC and the proposed approach. On user ID = 6, ours is completely consistent with the BHC. On user ID = 25, they are also identical, except that our group sensors 2 and 7 in a cluster while the BHC separates them and merges sensor 2 with a larger cluster. Clearly, the structures uncovered by the ODAC are quite distinct from those yielded by the BHC algorithm and although our partition on user ID = 25 is not consistent with that of the BHC, the overall results on two streams are considerably better than those of the ODAC.

In summary, the previously mentioned simulation demonstrates how, by exploiting the additional information, our approach leads to a substantial improvement in an emerging real-world application of temporal data clustering. However, a clustering ensemble with different representations naturally has a higher computational burden, requiring a slightly larger memory to perform the initial clustering analysis. Nevertheless, it is apparent from Fig. 7.3 that initial clustering analysis on different representations is a completely independent process, as is the generation of candidate consensus partitions. Thus, we hold that the highly advanced computing technology of today, for example, distributed computing, comprises adaptive capabilities which can help to overcome these weaknesses in a real-world application.

7.4 SUMMARY

If information loss during representation extraction is a fundamental weakness of representation-based temporal data clustering, the use of different temporal data representations in this proposed approach plays an important role in diminishing it.

Conceptually, temporal data representations acquired from different domains and on different scales tend to be complementary: temporal versus frequency, local versus global, and fine versus coarse. In the reported simulations, we simply use four complementary temporal data representations to demonstrate a method for cutting information loss. Our focus on representation-based clustering, however, has been somewhat to the detriment of representation-related issues per se, which includes the development of novel temporal data representations and how a synergy of representations can produce appropriate partitions for the clustering ensemble. We anticipate improvements to the proposed approach once these representation-related problems are tackled effectively.

The cost function derived in Eq. (7.9) suggests that the performance of a clustering ensemble depends both on the quality of input partitions and a sound clustering ensemble scheme. Initial clustering analysis is vital to performance. According to the first term of Eq. (7.9), good performance demands that the variance of input partitions is small and the optimal "mean" is close to the intrinsic "mean", that is, the ground-truth partition. Hence, clustering algorithms must first be appropriately matched to the nature of a given problem to produce such input partitions, aside from the use of different representations. Domain knowledge can be integrated via appropriate clustering algorithms during initial clustering analysis. Moreover, structural information underlying any given data set can be exploited, for example, by manifold clustering (Souvenir and Pless, 2005), to produce input partitions which reflect its intrinsic structure. As long as an initial clustering analysis returns input partitions which encode domain knowledge and characterize the intrinsic structural information, the "abstract" similarity (i.e., whether or not two entities are in the same cluster) used in our WCE will inherit them during the combination of input partitions. Additionally, the weighting scheme allows the integration of other useful criteria and domain knowledge, all of which suggests new ways to continue improving this proposed ensemble approach.

As shown, a clustering ensemble algorithm enables the flexible and effective use of different representations. Previous work (Chen et al., 1997; Chen, 1998; Chen and Chi, 1998; Chen, 2005a,b; Wang and Chen, 2007) demonstrates that a single learning model working on a composite representation formed by lumping different representations together is often inferior to an ensemble of multiple learning models on different representations in supervised and semisupervised learning. Moreover, our earlier empirical studies (Yang and Chen, 2006; Yang and Chen, 2007) and others not reported here, confirm our previous findings related to temporal data clustering. Thus, we believe that the proposed approach is both more effective and more efficient than a single learning model applied on the composite representation, which results in much higher dimension.

As a generic technique, our WCE algorithm is applicable to combinations of any input partitions in its own right, regardless of temporal data clustering. Therefore, we would link our algorithm to the most significant works and highlight the essential differences between them.

The CE algorithm (Strehl and Ghosh, 2003) presents three heuristic consensus functions for combining multiple partitions, which are applied to produce three candidate consensus partitions respectively. Then, the NMI criterion is employed to find a final partition by selecting, from the candidate partitions, the one of maximum NMI value. Although there is a two-stage reconciliation process in both their algorithm and ours, other factors clearly distinguish them from each other. First, ours uses only a uniform weighted consensus function, allowing various clustering validation criteria for weight generation. These criteria are used to produce multiple candidate consensus partitions (in this chapter, we use only three criteria). Then, we employ an agreement function to generate a final partition by combining all the candidate consensus partitions.

Our consensus and agreement functions are developed subject to the evidence accumulation framework (Fred and Jain, 2005). Unlike the original algorithm (Fred and Jain, 2005) where all input partitions are treated equally, we use the evidence accumulated in a selective way. When Eq. (7.10) is applied to the original algorithm (Fred and Jain, 2005) for analysis, it can be viewed as a special case of our algorithm as $w_m = 1/M$. Thus, its cost defined in Eq. (7.9) is simply a constant, independent of any combination. In other words, the algorithm (Fred and Jain, 2005) does not exploit useful information on the relationships between input partitions and works well only if all input partitions are of similar distance to the ground-truth partition in the partition space. Thus, we believe this analysis to expose the fundamental weakness of a clustering ensemble algorithm which treats all input partitions equally during the combination process.

Other WCE algorithms (Al-Razgan and Domeniconi, 2006; Cheng et al., 2008; Li and Ding, 2008) can, in general, be divided into two categories in terms of the weighting scheme: cluster or partition weighting. A cluster weighting scheme (Al-Razgan and Domeniconi, 2006; Cheng et al., 2008) associates the clusters in a partition with a weighting vector and embeds it in the subspace spanned by an adaptive combination of feature dimensions. A partition weighting scheme (Li and Ding, 2008) assigns a weight vector to the partitions to be combined. Our algorithm belongs to the latter category but adopts a different principle from that used by (Li and Ding, 2008) to generate weights.

The algorithm proposed by Li and Ding (2008) comes up with an objective function which encodes the overall weighted distance between all input partitions to be combined and the consensus partition to be found. Thus, an optimization problem has to be solved to find the optimal consensus partition. However, according to our analysis in Section 7.2.5, the optimal "mean" in terms of their objective function may be inconsistent with the optimal "mean" by minimizing the cost function defined in Eq. (7.8). Here, then, the quality of their consensus partition is not guaranteed. Although their algorithm is developed under the non-negative matrix factorization framework (Li and Ding, 2008), the iterative procedure for an optimal solution incurs a high computational complexity of O(n3). Our algorithm, by contrast, directly calculates weights with clustering validation criteria, allowing for the use of multiple criteria to measure the contribution of partitions, in turn leading to much faster computation. Indeed, the efficiency issue remains critical for several real-world applications, such as temporal data stream clustering. In our ongoing work, we are developing a weighting scheme to maximize the synergy between cluster and partition-based weighting.

To conclude, this chapter has presented a new temporal data clustering approach via a WCE on different representations and further proposed useful measures for understanding clustering ensemble algorithms based on formal clustering ensemble analysis (Topchy et al., 2004). The simulations have shown favorable results, in terms of clustering quality and model selection, for a variety of temporal data clustering tasks. Furthermore, as a generic framework, our approach allows for the direct incorporation of other validation criteria (Halkidi et al., 2001) to generate new weighting schemes, as long as the intrinsic structure underlying a data set would be better reflected. Finally, our approach does not involve a tedious parameter tuning process or bring with it a high level of computational complexity. It is a promising yet easy-to-use technique, designed for real-world applications.

Conclusions, Future Work

8

The works presented in this book principally focus on solving the fundamental problems of temporal data clustering tasks in close association with ensemble-learning techniques. As described earlier, there are three methodologies for temporal data clustering; model-based clustering, proximity-based clustering, and feature-based clustering. Each approach favors differently structured temporal data or types of temporal data with certain assumptions. There is nothing universal that can solve all problems, and it is important to understand the characteristics of both clustering algorithms and the target temporal data, so that the right approach can be selected for a given clustering problem. However, there are very limited amounts of prior information for most clustering tasks, making the selection of a proper clustering algorithm for certain characteristics of temporal data extremely difficult. Therefore, motivated by the divide-and-conquer principle (Chen, 2005), the research has been carried out over a range of aspects of the three categorized temporal-clustering approaches: model-based clustering, proximity-based clustering, and feature-based clustering. Using a wide range of background knowledge and supportive study, we identify each approach's different characteristics based on their strengths and weaknesses. Model-based approaches such as Hidden Markov Model (HMM) have outstanding ability in modeling the dynamic behaviors of temporal data, but they critically suffer from detecting the intrinsic number of clusters as model-selection problem and high computational costs. Although the proximity-based approach gives a simple method for directly applying conventional static data—clustering algorithms to temporal data with appropriate similarity measures, it still presents a real challenge in general temporal data—clustering tasks due to several distinct characteristics of temporal data, such as its high dimensionality, complex time dependency, and large volume (Sun and Giles, 2000). Representation-based approaches reduce the computational complexities for high dimensional temporal data. However, in normal circumstances, the process of feature extraction always causes the loss of information in the original temporal data, and extracted features cannot fully capture the characteristics of temporal data. Furthermore, the model-selection problem remains critical. In order to overcome the problems inherent in these temporal-clustering approaches, three clustering ensemble models have been specifically proposed by author, and the experimental results reported in this book demonstrate the robustness and feasibility of the proposed solutions.

Initially we proposed a novel *HMM-based meta-clustering ensemble* model from the perspective of a model-based approach, which consists of three modules; flat partitional clustering, a clustering ensemble, and finally, agglomerative meta-clustering. In the flat partitional clustering module, various partitions of target temporal data are generated by HMM-based K-models clustering (Butler, 2003) with different model initializations. In the clustering ensemble module, three consensus functions Cluster-based Similarity Partitioning Algorithm (CSPA), Hyper-Graph partitioning Algorithm (HGPA), and Meta-CLustering Algorithm (MCLA) (Strehl and Ghosh, 2003) are individually applied, combining the collection of multiple partitions in forming the final partition candidates from different perspectives. Moreover, the mutual information-based objective (Strehl and Ghosh, 2003) is used to determine an optimal partition, the final ensemble partition, from these candidates. Then, applying the proposed Dendrogram-based Similarity Partitioning Algorithm (DSPA) consensus function (Yang and Chen, 2006) on target temporal data, the intrinsic number of clusters is automatically determined. In the final module of HMM-agglomerative clustering, by use of the symmetric version of *Boundary*KL distance measure, the intercluster distance is calculated and compared. The closest pair of clusters is merged to form a composite model. The process of merging clusters is repeated until a determined number of clusters is reached. This model-based clustering ensemble approach results in four major benefits:

1. No parameter re-estimation is required for the new merged pair of clusters, significantly reducing computation costs, which has been typically justified in a similar model-based hybrid-clustering approach proposed by Zhong and Ghosh (2003). As described in Section 5.2.2, the clusters of optimal consensus partition obtained from clustering ensemble are treated as meta-data, then standard HMM-based agglomerative clustering is applied to group the meta-data, where the distance between meta-data as intercluster distance is calculated and compared by using the symmetric version of *Boundary*KL distance measure, the closest pair of clusters is merged to form a composite model concatenating the model parameters of each clusters instead of re-estimating the parameters of merged clusters.

2. In comparison to single model such as HMM-based hybrid partitional-hierarchical clustering, the composite model is better equipped to characterize complexly structured clusters in order to produce a robust and accurate clustering results, which has been demonstrated on a various temporal data sets including HMM-generated data set shown in Table 5.1, a general synthetic data set (CBF) shown in Table 5.2, and a collection of time series benchmarks shown in Table 5.4.

3. The model initialization problem is solved by implementing the ensemble technique, which has been typically investigated by an experimental study described in Section 5.3 on both of HMM-generated data set and a general

synthetic data set (CBF) in comparison with other similar model-based clustering algorithms. As shown in Tables 5.1 and 5.2, the higher averaged classification accuracy with smaller standard deviation obtained by the proposed approach just demonstrated its insensitivity to model initialization.

4. The appropriate cluster number (model selection) can be automatically determined by applying a proposed consensus function DSPA (Yang and Chen, 2006) on multiple partitions of the target temporal data during the ensemble process. This automatic model selection ability has been systematically testified on HMM-generated data set shown in Fig. 5.2, a general synthetic data set (CBF) shown in Fig. 5.5, and a collection of time series benchmark shown in Table 5.4. Compared with standard model selection approach Bayesian information criterion (BIC) on HMM-generated data set shown in Fig. 5.3 and a general synthetic data set (CBF) shown in Fig. 5.6, the better performance of our proposed ensemble model has become obvious.

Although this algorithm is able to reduce the computational cost in the final module of agglomerative clustering due to no parameter re-estimation for composite models, it is still quite time consuming in comparison with other proposed algorithms, which has been systematically analyzed in computational complexity and further demonstrated on CAVIAR database shown in Table 7.4.

Therefore, we proposed an *Iteratively constructed clustering ensemble* in order to reduce the computational cost and provide a meaningful combination of input partitions by a hybrid sampling technique. Basically this approach iteratively constructs multiple partitions on the subset of whole input instances, selected by a hybrid combination of boosting and bagging sampling schemes. Weights over instances are updated for each iteration, and part of the subtraining set is chosen according to weights over instances as a selection probability. The rest of the subtraining set is constructed using random sampling from the input space. Then, a basic clustering algorithm is applied to partition the subtraining set, and the final output of the clustering ensemble is obtained by aggregating this iterative construction. Four major benefits become very clear:

1. By subsampling, computational costs are significantly reduced during the training process, which has been demonstrated by a comparison of three proposed clustering ensemble models based on computational complexity and execution time on motion trajectories database (CAVIAR) shown in Table 7.4.

2. There is an improved diversity of input partitions obtained from the training subset. As shown in Figs. 6.1 and 6.3, a *Normalized Mutual Information (NMI)* criterion has been used to measure diversity of input partitions produced by the proposed approach, restarted K-means, bagging and boosting, respectively, on Gaussian-generated data set and a general synthetic data set (CBF).

3. For complex-structured data set such as time series and large data set, the major strengths of both boosting and bagging are greatly employed for solving clustering problems, where dealing with clustered data with unbalanced populations, arbitrary shapes, and large volume are simplified by sampling

techniques, and certain difficult problems are divided into several interacted simple tasks. It has been initially demonstrated on a Gaussian-generated 2D-data set as the motivation described in Section 6.2.1 and a general synthetic data set (CBF) with a visualization and better understanding on the experiment results shown in Figs. 6.1 and 6.3, respectively. Then a set of experiments on time series benchmarks shown in Table 6.2 and motion trajectories database (CAVIAR) shown in Fig. 6.6 were carried out in Section 6.3. The experimental results have demonstrated that the proposed algorithms generally have a better performance than either boosting or bagging algorithm.

4. We can directly apply most conventional static data clustering algorithms as a base learner. As a general framework for ensemble learning, hierarchical, K-NN, and K-means have been employed as the base learner of the proposed clustering ensemble model; each of them has shown the promising results on a collection of time series benchmark in Table 6.2.

However, this proposed clustering ensemble model has the major difficulty of dealing with the data sets with various lengths, which requires the data sets to be uniform length, and combining the input partitions with different number of clusters, where the input partitions must have identical number of clusters due to the limitation of majority voting combination.

Finally, we proposed a *Weighted clustering ensemble with multiple representations* in order to provide an alternative solution to solve the common problems such as selection of intrinsic cluster numbers, computational cost, and combination method raised by both former proposed clustering ensemble models from the perspective of a feature-based approach. The approach consists of three phases of work. First, temporal data are transformed into a different feature space and become the input for the clustering algorithm. Second, the clustering algorithm is applied for clustering analyses. Finally, clustering ensemble on different representations are employed, and the weighted consensus function, based on three different clustering validity criterion—Modified Huber's T Index (Theodoridis et al., 1999), Dunn's Validity Index (Davies and Bouldin, 1979), and NMI (Vinh et al., 2009)—is carried out to find out an optimal single consensus partition from multiple partitions based on different representations. Then, a final agreement function is used to construct the final partition from the candidates yielded by the weighted consensus function based on different clustering validity criterion. This proposed representation-based clustering ensemble model results in four major benefits:

1. Through representation, the complex structures of temporal data with variable length and high dimensionality are transformed into lower-fixed dimensional feature spaces, significantly reducing computational burden, which has been demonstrated on the motion trajectories database (CAVIAR) in terms of execution time shown in Table 7.4.

2. We see a high capability for capturing the properties of temporal data as well as the synergy of reconciling diverse partitions with different representations, which has been initially demonstrated on a synthetic 2D-data set as the motivation described in Section 7.2.1 with a visualization and better understanding on the experiment results shown in Fig. 7.1. Moreover, a set of experiments on time series benchmark shown in Table 7.1 and motion trajectories database (CAVIAR) shown in Fig. 7.5 demonstrated the benefit of using different representations in comparison of solely using single representation.

3. The weighted consensus function has outstanding ability in automatic model selection and appropriate grouping for complex temporal data, which has been initially demonstrated on a complex Gaussian-generated 2D-data set shown in Fig. 7.2 as the motivation described in Section 7.2.1, then a set of experiments on time series benchmarks shown in Table 7.1 in comparison with standards temporal data clustering algorithms, Table 7.2 in comparison with three state-of-the-art ensemble learning algorithms, Table 7.3 in comparison with other proposed clustering ensemble models on motion trajectories database (CAVIAR).

4. There is enhanced flexibility in association with most of existing clustering algorithms. As a general framework for ensemble learning, K-means, hierarchical, and Density-Based Spatial Clustering of Applications with Noise (DBSCAN) have been employed as the base learner of this proposed clustering ensemble model; each of them has shown the promising results on a collection of time series benchmark shown in Table 7.1. Also the proposed clustering ensemble model has been successfully applied for online time-series data streaming clustering, which has demonstrated on the Physiological Data Modeling Contest Workshop data set in Table 7.6 and Fig. 7.7.

Although there are some achievements made on the temporal data mining during last decade, there remain several open theoretical questions we can try to answer and research directions to follow in the future.

1. From the perspective of representation-based temporal clustering, the exploration of effective yet complementary representations in association with the clustering ensemble is a difficult task when applied to various structured temporal data.

2. For model-based temporal clustering, it is clearly important to choose a suitable model family, for example, the HMM, a mixture of first-order Markov chain (Smyth, 1999), dynamic Bayesian networks (Murphy, 2002), or the autoregressive moving average model (Xiong and Yeung, 2002). The choice is made according to the best representation of differently structured temporal data. Subsequently constructed is the suitable similarity measure applied to the specified model family. Moreover, Expectation Maximization (EM) algorithm (Chang, 2002) is used for model parameter estimation, causing problems of local optima and convergence difficulty.

3. With a discrete optimization problem approach, during each run of the clustering ensemble, the base learner constructs a "best" partition on the subset of the target data set (subsampling) by optimizing a predefined clustering quality

measure. However, the appropriate partition will better approximate the underlying data space of the target data set (ground truth) than will the "best" partition, which is treated as an over fitting problem.

4. The clustering objective function (clustering quality measure) is the core of any clustering algorithm. It is extremely difficult to design such internal criterion without supervision information.

5. An effective data clustering approach requires a minimum amount of user-dependent parameters. However, most current clustering algorithms always require several key input parameters in order to produce optimal clustering results. They are, therefore, unfeasible for use in real-world applications.

Appendix

A.1 WEIGHTED CLUSTERING ENSEMBLE ALGORITHM ANALYSIS

This appendix comprises empirical studies on the capabilities and limitations of our weighted clustering ensemble (WCE) algorithm based on the algorithm analysis described in Section 7.2.5.

As pointed out in Section 7.2.5, the Eq. (7.10) critically determines the performance of our WCE via the quantities $|\mu_m - w_m|$. As a result, we need both μ_m and w_m for a given data set $X = \{\mathbf{x}_n\}_{n=1}^N$. While w_m is achieved by applying a clustering validation criteria or a combination of them to the input partitions, μ_m is generally unavailable unless we know both the ground-truth partition and all possible partitions of the given data set.

In reality, there is only a subset of partitions, $\mathbf{P} = \{P_m\}_{m=1}^M$, returned by initial clustering analysis (ICA). We approximate μ_m using only these partitions through a partition similarity measure, the Normalized Mutual Information (NMI) although other similarity measures can also be used. Thus, we estimate μ_m corresponding to P_m by,

$$\widehat{\mu}_m = \frac{\mathrm{NMI}(P_m, P_c)}{\sum_{m=1}^M \mathrm{NMI}(P_m, P_c)} \tag{A.1}$$

where P_c is the ground-truth partition of X and

$$\mathrm{NMI}(P_m, P_c) = \frac{\sum_{i=1}^{K_m} \sum_{j=1}^{K_c} N_{ij}^{mc} \log\left(\frac{N N_{ij}^{mc}}{N_i^a N_j^b}\right)}{\sum_{i=1}^{K_m} N_i^m \log\left(\frac{N_i^m}{N}\right) + \sum_{j=1}^{K_c} N_j^c \log\left(\frac{N_j^c}{N}\right)}. \tag{A.2}$$

Here, K_m and K_c are the number of clusters in P_m and P_c, respectively. N_{ij}^{mc} is the number of entities shared by the clusters $C_i^m \in P_m$ and $C_j^c \in P_c$, where there are N_i^m and N_j^c entities in C_i^m and C_j^c.

As described in Section 7.2.3, three clustering validation criteria are employed to generate weights but do not combine three weighted similarity matrices directly. Instead, we combine only the three optimal partitions yielded by cutting dendrogram trees constructed with three weighted similarity matrices at the longest lifetime. Strictly speaking, the similarity matrix of the final consensus partition becomes a binary version of the multiple criteria—based weighted similarity matrix by applying a threshold. Nevertheless, we firmly believe that this binary version inherits most characteristics of the original multiple criteria—based weighted similarity matrix. Hence, we approximate its weight by,

$$\overline{w}_m = \frac{1}{3} \sum_\pi w_m^\pi, \tag{A.3}$$

where $\pi = \{$DVI, MHT, NMI$\}$ defined in Section 3.3.

In general, data distribution and underlying cluster shapes may be arbitrarily complex. Therefore, it is impossible to examine all possible data sets exhaustively. In this empirical studies, we employ two of the most important cluster properties, compactness and separability, as guidelines for the production of data sets. As the Gaussian mixture model (GMM) can approximate any kind of distribution, we employ the GMM of four Gaussian components to produce data sets of four clusters ($K^* = 4$). By altering parameters, mean, covariance, and mixture proportion in the GMM, we can produce data sets of different data distributions and cluster shapes. For visualization purposes, we have produced three 2D data sets of clearly distinct properties.

In this experiments, we use K-mean in the ICA. The procedure clearly described in Section 7.3.1. K is randomly chosen from a range $1 \leq K \leq 8$, and 20 partitions are produced under different initial conditions for a given data set. We name such an initial clustering analysis, ICA1. To simulate the limitations of ICA, we also use another range of K: $1 \leq K \leq 8$ and $K \neq K^*$ to produce 20 partitions for a given data set. We denote such an ICA as an ICA2. The purpose of this simulation is twofold: to investigate the capacities and limitations of our WCE and to verify the benefits of using multiple validation indexes (MVIs).

As shown in Fig. A.1A, data set 1 can be viewed as a representative of a class of data sets that have tight compactness and high separability, a good class of data sets for clustering analysis. Such properties should be easily captured with any clustering validation criterion. As observed in Fig. A.1B and C, our WCE based on the MVI yields almost perfect partitions, even when the ICA returns no correct partitions, given that there are no partitions on four clusters retuned by ICA2. As expected, the use of a single criterion in the WCE is enough to produce satisfactory partitions, as illustrated in Fig. A.1D—I with the exception of Fig. A.1H. However, a single criterion is not robust enough against inadequate ICA, as demonstrated in Fig. A.1H, where the WCE based on the MHT criterion fails to produce a correct partition. Fig. A.1J and K show little similarity between the ideal weight and the ground-truth partition μ_m, defined in Eq. A.1 and a weight based on one or more clustering validation criteria w_m collectively. From Fig. A.1J and K it is clear that any dissimilarity between μ_m and $\overline{w}_m$ defined in Eq. A.3, is much smaller than any dissimilarity between μ_m and w_m^π overall, while dissimilarity between μ_m and w_m^π, $\pi = \{$DVI, MHT, NMI$\}$) varies

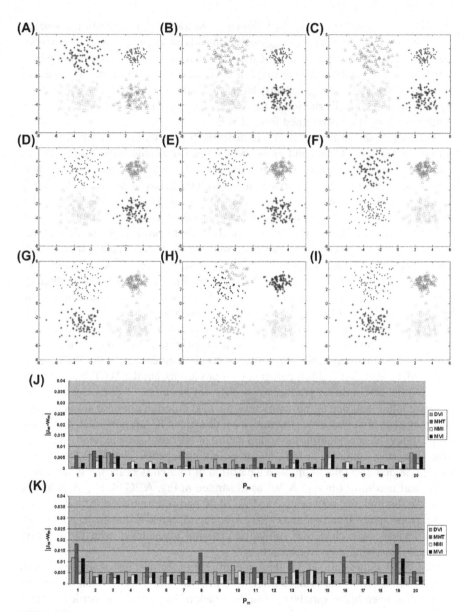

FIGURE A.1

Results on data set 1. (A) Ground truth. (B) Partition by WCE based on multiple validation indexes (K-means, $1 \leq k \leq 8$). (C) Partition by WCE based on multiple validation indexes (K-means, $1 \leq k \leq 8$ and $K \neq 4$). (D)–(F) Partitions by WCE based on DVI, MHT, and NMI (K-means, $1 \leq k \leq 8$). (G)–(I) Partitions by WCE based on DVI, MHT, and NMI (K-means, $1 \leq k \leq 8$ and $K \neq 4$). (J) Dissimilarity between w_m and μ_m of 20 partitions (K-means, $1 \leq k \leq 8$). (K) Dissimilarity between w_m and μ_m of 20 partitions (K-means, $1 \leq k \leq 8$ and $K \neq 4$) (Yang and Chen, 2011a).

across 20 partitions. Equation 7.10 shown in Section 7.2.5 suggests the smaller collective dissimilarity between μ_m and w_m results in a lower cost. These experimental results confirm the benefit of using MVI to measure the contribution of a partition for combination. In addition, Fig. A1K shows that the overall dissimilarity between μ_m and w_m^{MHT} is significantly larger than others. This explains why restricting the use of the MHT criterion to the WCE fails to produce a correct partition by combining 20 partitions returned from ICA2.

Data set 2, shown in Fig. A.2A, is different from data set 1 in the number of entities in different clusters and in its compact and separable state. Alongside this data set's identifiable properties, the intracluster variability gets higher and the intercluster variability becomes lower, in contrast with the behavior of data set 1, leading to a more difficult clustering analysis task. In Fig. A.2B and C, our WCE yields a satisfactory partition, detecting the correct number of clusters by combining partitions returned by ICA1. The WCE equally fails to produce a partition of the intrinsic structure by combining partitions returned by ICA2. The ambiguity arises when separability between different clusters is low. Incorrect ICA inevitably misleads the clustering ensemble into producing an incorrect partition due to ambiguity. This result suggests that ICA plays a critical role, particularly when there appears to be low separability between different clusters. In other words, a clustering ensemble itself cannot detect the intrinsic structure underlying a data set unless input partitions carry such information. As these ambiguities appear, the WCE based on a single criterion is no longer reliable. From Fig. A.2D–F, it emerges that the WCE based on the MHT criterion yields a partition of four clusters but the WCE based on the DVI and the NMI criteria produces two different partitions of three clusters. This in turn implies that, due to this ambiguity, a single criterion does not always recognize partitions of the intrinsic structure, even though an ICA returns such partitions. Again, this evidence confirms the sound nature of our motivation to jointly use multiple clustering validation criteria in our weighting scheme. The WCE based on a single criterion also fails to produce a partition of four clusters for the same reason as the partition shown in Fig. A.2C, as illustrated in Fig. A.2G–I. Fig. A.2J and K show the dissimilarity between μ_m and w_m of 20 partitions returned from ICA1 and ICA2, respectively. It can be seen clearly from Fig. A.2J and K that the larger dissimilarity appears as a clustering validation criterion mismatches with the intrinsic structure underlying a given data set.

Fig. A.3A shows data set 3 with no identifiable properties, full of ambiguity, and without reference to the ground truth. In particular, intracluster variability is far higher than intercluster variability. Due to a lack of identifiable properties, neither a clustering algorithm nor a clustering validation criterion works on such a data set. As anticipated, the WCE based on either a single criterion or the multiple criteria fails to yield a partition close to the ground truth, as shown in Fig. A.3B–I. Our weight dissimilarity index values, illustrated in Fig. A.3J and K, also clearly indicate the reason for failure.

In summary, these experimental results suggest that our WCE, based on multiple validation criteria, performs well but relies heavily on the quality of input partitions

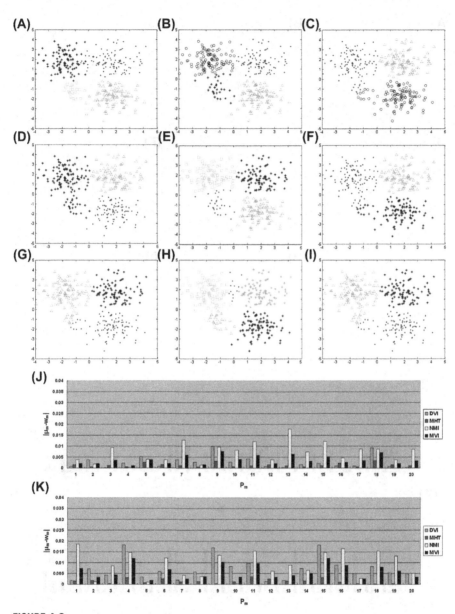

FIGURE A.2

Results on data set 2. (A) Ground truth. (B) Partition by WCE based on multiple validation indexes (K-means, $1 \leq k \leq 8$). (C) Partition by WCE based on multiple validation indexes (K-means, $1 \leq k \leq 8$ and $K \neq 4$). (D)–(F) Partitions by WCE based on DVI, MHT, and NMI (K-means, $1 \leq k \leq 8$). (G)–(I) Partitions by WCE based on DVI, MHT, and NMI (K-means, $1 \leq k \leq 8$ and $K \neq 4$). (J) Dissimilarity between w_m and μ_m of 20 partitions (K-means, $1 \leq k \leq 8$). (K) Dissimilarity between w_m and μ_m of 20 partitions (K-means, $1 \leq k \leq 8$ and $K \neq 4$) (Yang and Chen, 2011a).

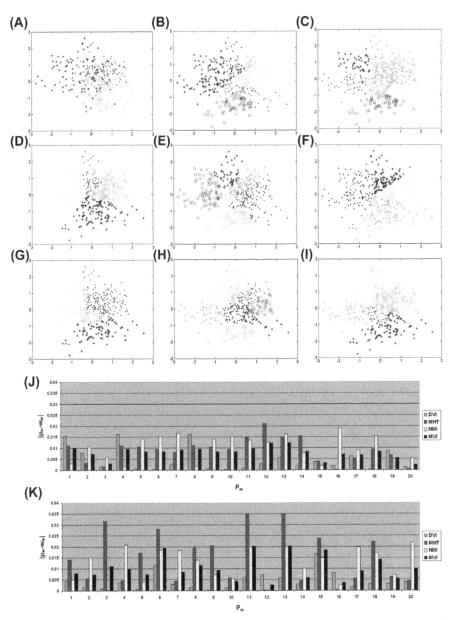

FIGURE A.3

Results on data set 3. (A) Ground truth. (B) Partition by WCE based on multiple validation indexes (K-means, $1 \leq k \leq 8$). (C) Partition by WCE based on multiple validation indexes (K-means, $1 \leq k \leq 8$ and $K \neq 4$). (D)–(F) Partitions by WCE based on DVI, MHT, and NMI (K-means, $1 \leq k \leq 8$). (G)–(I) Partitions by WCE based on DVI, MHT, and NMI (K-means, $1 \leq k \leq 8$ and $K \neq 4$). (J) Dissimilarity between w_m and μ_m of 20 partitions (K-means, $1 \leq k \leq 8$). (K) Dissimilarity between w_m and μ_m of 20 partitions (K-means, $1 \leq k \leq 8$ and $K \neq 4$) (Yang and Chen, 2011a).

returned by ICA, in particular when a given data set contains less identifiable structural information about the cluster. This could mean situations of low separability, uneven cluster size, high intracluster, or low interclass variability. In general, this empirical studies are consistent with algorithm analysis presented in Section 7.2.5. As demonstrated in plots J and K of Figs. A.1–A.3, the dissimilarity between the optimal "weights" μ_m and "weights" w_m, generated via clustering validation criteria, becomes a useful measure by which to understand the behaviors of our WCE algorithm as applied to different data sets. These results also demonstrate the benefits of using multiple clustering validation criteria in our weighting scheme when the ground truth is not available.

A.2 IMPLEMENTATION OF HMM-BASED META-CLUSTERING ENSEMBLE IN MATLAB CODE

```
load('data');
size(data)
Sn=2;  %number of states
cyc=6; %number of HMM estimation cycles
for p=1:10    %generating partitions
  fprintf('partitioning.%d .....\n', p);
  [ctr,gs]=hmmkm(data,Sn,cyc);
  cls(p,:)=gs;
end
% Perform clustering ensemble
[cl cluster_n]=clusterensemble(cls);
% Perform HMM-based Agglomerative clustering
g=hmmagg(data,cl,cluster_n,Sn,cyc); %%%%%%%%%%%%%%%%%%%%%%%%%%%%%%%%
function [ctr,g]=hmmkm(m,Sn,cyc)
[maxN maxD]=size(m);
p = randperm(size(m,1));  % random initialization
k=4+ceil(4*3)-1;    % select k (k*=4)
for i=1:k
  trx=m(p(i),:);
  smp(i,:)=trx;
  [Nm Dim]=size(trx);
  trx=reshape(trx',Dim*Nm,1);
  [Mu,Cov,P,Pi,LL]=hmm_est(trx,Dim,Sn,cyc);
  hmm(i)=struct('LL',LL,'Pi',Pi,'P',P,'Mu',Mu,'Cov',Cov);
end
temp=zeros(maxN,1);  % initialize as zero vector
cnt =0;
while 1
  d=DisMatrix(m,hmm,smp,Sn); % calculate distances matrix
  [z,g]=max(d,[],2); % find group matrix g
```

```
        if g==temp | cnt==5,
          break;        % stop the iteration
        else
          temp=g;        % copy group matrix to temporary variable
        end
        for i=1:k
          f=find(g==i);
          if f % only compute centroid if f is not empty
            trx=m((find(g==i)),:);
            [Nm Dim]=size(trx);
            trx=reshape(trx',Dim*Nm,1);
            [Mu,Cov,P,Pi,LL]=hmm_est(trx,Dim,Sn,cyc);
            hmm(i)=struct('LL',LL,'Pi',Pi,'P',...
              P,'Mu',Mu,'Cov',Cov);
          end
        end
        cnt=cnt+1;
      end
      ctr=hmm;
      end
%%%%%%%%%%%%%%%%%%%%%%%%%%%%%%%%%%%%%%%%%%%%%%%%%%%%%%%%%%%%%
function d=DisMatrix(m,hmm,smp,Sn)
Nb=size(m,1);
Kc=size(hmm,2);
for n=1:Nb
  for k=1:Kc
    trx=m(n,:);
    [Nm Dim]=size(trx);
    trx=reshape(trx',Dim*Nm,1);
    [lik,likv]=hmm_cl(trx,Dim,Sn,hmm(k).Mu,...
      hmm(k).Cov,hmm(k).P,hmm(k).Pi);
    d(n,k)=lik;
  end
end
%%%%%%%%%%%%%%%%%%%%%%%%%%%%%%%%%%%%%%%%%%%%%%%%%%%%%%%%%%%%%
function [cl dcn]= clusterensemble(cls)
if size(cls,2)>1000,
  workfcts = {'hgpa', 'mcla'};
  disp('clusterensemble-warning: using only hgpa and mcla');
  for i = 1:length(workfcts);
    workfct = workfcts{i};
    if ~exist('k'),
      cl(i,:) = feval(workfct,cls);
    else
      cl(i,:) = feval(workfct,cls,k);
    end;
    q(i) = ceevalmutual(cls,cl(i,:));
    disp(['clusterensemble: ' workfct ' at ' num2str(q(i))]);
  end;
```

```
else
  workfcts = {'cspa', 'hgpa', 'mcla'};
  for i = 1:length(workfcts);
    workfct = workfcts{i};
    if ~exist('k'),
      cl(i,:) = feval(workfct,cls);
    else
      cl(i,:) = feval(workfct,cls,k);
    end;
    q(i) = ceevalmutual(cls,cl(i,:));
    disp(['clusterensemble: ' workfct ' at ' num2str(q(i))]);
  end;
end;
[qual, best] = max(q);
cl = cl(best,:);
cl=relabel(cl);
dcl = DSPA(cls);
dcl=relabel(dcl);
dcn=length(unique(dcl)); % automatically detect on by DSPA
%%%%%%%%%%%%%%%%%%%%%%%%%%%%%%%%%%%%%%%%%%%%%%%%%%%%%%%%%%%%%%
function cl=relabel(g)
idx=unique(g);
idxn=length(idx);
for cn=1:idxn
  cl(find(g==idx(cn)))=cn;
end
%%%%%%%%%%%%%%%%%%%%%%%%%%%%%%%%%%%%%%%%%%%%%%%%%%%%%%%%%%%%%%
function label = DSPA(cls)
clbs = clstoclbs(cls);
s = clbs' * clbs;
s = checks(s./size(cls,1));
n=size(s,1);
x=ones(n,n);
s=x-s;
Y=[];
for j=1:n-1
Y=[Y,s(j,(j+1):n)];
end
Z= linkage(Y,'complete');
[h w]=size(Z);
for i=1:h-1
lifetime(i)=Z(i+1,w)-Z(i,w);
end
ma=find(lifetime==max(lifetime));
thres=Z(ma,w)+(Z(ma+1,w)-Z(ma,w))*rand;
[H,T] = dendrogram(Z,0,'colorthreshold',thres(1));
clu=cluster(Z,'CUTOFF',thres,'CRITERION','distance');
label=clu';
%%%%%%%%%%%%%%%%%%%%%%%%%%%%%%%%%%%%%%%%%%%%%%%%%%%%%%%%%%%%%%
```

```
function g=hmmagg(m,cl,cluster_n,Sn,cyc)
k=length(unique(cl));
Y=[];
g=cl;
% re-estimate the models parameters in consensus partition
for i=1:k
  trx=m((find(cl==i)),:);
  smp(i,:)=mean(trx,1);
  [Nm Dim]=size(trx);
  trx=reshape(trx',Dim*Nm,1);
  [Mu,Cov,P,Pi,LL]=hmm_est(trx,Dim,Sn,cyc);
  hmm(i)=struct('LL',LL,'Pi',Pi,'P',...
    P,'Mu',Mu,'Cov',Cov);
end
% construct composite model by merging the close models
d=DisMatrix(m,hmm,smp,Sn);
for L1=1:k-1
  for L2=L1+1:k
    idx=find(cl==L1|cl==L2);
    kld=sum(abs(d(idx,L1)-d(idx,L2)))/length(idx);
    Y=[Y,kld];
  end
end
Z= linkage(Y,'average');
clu = cluster(Z,'MaxClust',cluster_n);
for j=1:length(clu);
  g(find(cl==j))=clu(j);
end
%%%%%%%%%%%%%%%%%%%%%%%%%%%%%%%%%%%%%%%%%%%%%%%%%%%%%%%%%%%%%%%%
% The other functions related to clustering ensemble(ClusterEnsemble
% Toolbox) are downloaded
% http://www.lans.ece.utexas.edu/~strehl/soft.html

% The other functions related to HMM(Machine Learning Toolbox) are
% downloaded
% http://mlg.eng.cam.ac.uk/zoubin/software.html
```

A.3 IMPLEMENTATION OF ITERATIVELY CONSTRUCTED CLUSTERING ENSEMBLE IN MATLAB CODE

```
load('data');
k=5;  %k*=5
weak_learner_n = 10;
% Perform Iteratively constructed clustering ensemble model
[outputs g]= ICCE(@b_partition,data',weak_learner_n,k);
%%%%%%%%%%%%%%%%%%%%%%%%%%%%%%%%%%%%%%%%%%%%%%%%%%%%%%%%%%%%%%%%%
```

```
function [B_model Lag]= ICCE(tr_func_handle, train_set, ...
   no_of_hypothesis,k)
Lag=[];
buf=[];
[B_model Lag] = struct('weights',zeros(1,no_of_hypothesis),...
  'parameters',[]);
sample_n = size(train_set,1);
samples_weight = ones(sample_n,1)/sample_n;
for turn=1:no_of_hypothesis
  fprintf('Interation %d \n',turn);
  B_model.parameters{turn} = ...
    tr_func_handle(train_set,samples_weight,k,turn);
  CQ=B_model.parameters{turn}.CQ;
  H(:,:,turn)=B_model.parameters{turn}.hypo;
  [z,L]=max(H(:,:,turn),[],2);
  % solving the correspondence problem
  if turn>1
    similarity_matrix = NaN(max(Lag),max(L));
    for i = 1 : max(Lag)
      for j = 1 : max(L)
        Ci = find(Lag == i);
        Cj = find(L == j);
        similarity_matrix(i, j) = 2 * length(intersect(Ci, Cj))
          /(length(Ci) + length(Cj));
      end
    end
    sim=exp(-similarity_matrix);
    [assignment,cost] = munkres(sim);
    H(:,:,turn)=B_model.parameters{turn}.hypo(:,assignment);
    [z,L]=max(H(:,:,turn),[],2);
  end
  % calculating the cost(error) at turn
  err=sum(CQ.*samples_weight)/2;
  E(turn)=err;
  B(turn)=(1-err)/err;
  % The weight of the turn-th base learner
  B_model.weights = log10(B)/sum(log10(B));
  % Update the training data weights Wi
  samples_weight = samples_weight.*(B(turn).^CQ);
  % Normalization weights Wi
  samples_weight = samples_weight/sum(samples_weight);
  % Compute the aggregate cluster hypothesis Hag, and partition Lag
  for c=1:turn
    buf(:,:,turn)=H(:,:,turn).*B_model.weights(turn);
  end
  Hag=sum(buf,3);
  [z,Lag]=max(Hag,[],2);
  % Compute the loss of final partition
  en_CQ=1-max(Hag,[],2)+min(Hag,[],2);
  loss(turn)=sum(en_CQ.*samples_weight)/2;
end
%%%%%%%%%%%%%%%%%%%%%%%%%%%%%%%%%%%%%%%%%%%%%%%%%%%%%%%%%%%%%%%%%%%%%%
```

```
function model = b_partition(train_set,sample_weights,k,turn)
model = struct('hypo',[],'CQ',[]);
train_n = size(train_set,1);
sample_n= floor(train_n/10);
% a hybrid sampling
if turn==1
  sample_set=train_set(randi(train_n ,1,sample_n),:);
else
  sample_idx = SampleDistribution(floor(sample_n/2),...
    sample_weights);
  floor(sample_n/2);
  r_train_set=train_set;
  r_train_set(sample_idx,:)=[];
  r_train_n = size(r_train_set,1);
  buf=randperm(r_train_n);
  sampidx=buf(1:(sample_n-floor(sample_n/2)));
  sample_set=[train_set(sample_idx,:);r_train_set(sampidx,:)];
end
[y,ctr,g]=kMeansCluster(sample_set,k); %Apply k-means
d=DistMatrix(train_set,ctr);
[l w]=size(d);
%%%%calculate Hij
for i=1:l
  m1=repmat(d(i,:)',1,k);
  m2=ones(k,1)./d(i,:)';
  h(i,:)= ones(1,k)./(m1*m2)';
end
[z,L]=max(h,[],2);
%%% calculate CQi
model.hypo=h;
model.CQ=1-max(h,[],2)+min(h,[],2);
%%%%%%%%%%%%%%%%%%%%%%%%%%%%%%%%%%%%%%%%%%%%%%%%%%%%%%%%%%%%%%%%%%
function ret_vec = SampleDistribution(num_samples, pdf)
CumDist = cumsum(pdf);
num_samples_per = 10;
num_finish_sample = 0;
while num_finish_sample < num_samples
  % decide how many to sample each time
  if num_samples > num_finish_sample + num_samples_per
    num_to_sample = num_samples_per;
  else
    num_to_sample = num_samples - num_finish_sample;
  end
  % sample out num_to_sample examples
   Diff = CumDist * ones(1, num_to_sample) - ones(length(pdf), 1) * rand(1,
num_to_sample);
  Diff = (Diff <= 0) * 2 + Diff;
  [C, I] = min(Diff);
```

```
  % accumulate the sample_vec
  if num_finish_sample == 0
    ret_vec = I';
  else
    ret_vec = [ret_vec; I'];
  end
  num_finish_sample = num_finish_sample + num_to_sample;
end
%%%%%%%%%%%%%%%%%%%%%%%%%%%%%%%%%%%%%%%%%%%%%%%%%%%%%%%%%%%%%%%%
function d=DistMatrix(A,B)
[hA,wA]=size(A);
[hB,wB]=size(B);
for n=1:hA
  for k=1:hB
    a=sum((A(n,:)-B(k,:)).^2);
    d(n,k)=a;
  end
end
%%%%%%%%%%%%%%%%%%%%%%%%%%%%%%%%%%%%%%%%%%%%%%%%%%%%%%%%%%%%%%%%
% Hungarian Algorithm ([ASSIGN,COST] = munkres(COSTMAT)) is
% downloaded
% http://www.mathworks.com/matlabcentral/fileexchange/20652-
% hungarian-algorithm-for-linear-assignment-problems-v2-2/
% content/munkre%s.m
```

A.4 IMPLEMENTATION OF WCE WITH DIFFERENT REPRESENTATIONS

```
load('data');
x = f_extract(data,1); %representation PCF
cls1=partition_ensm(x,10); %generating partitions
y= f_extract(data,2); %representation DFT
cls2=partition_ensm(y,10); %generating partitions
z = f_extract(data,3); %representation PLS
cls3=partition_ensm(z,10); %generating partitions
w = f_extract(data,4); %representation PDWT
cls4=partition_ensm(w,10); %generating partitions
cls=[cls1;cls2;cls3;cls4];
g = WCE(cls,data'); %perform Weighted clustering ensemble
%%%%%%%%%%%%%%%%%%%%%%%%%%%%%%%%%%%%%%%%%%%%%%%%%%%%%%%%%%%%%%%%
function reps = f_extract(x,opt)
if opt==1   %representation PCF
  [Hx,Wx]=size(x);
  t=1:Wx;
  t=(t-mean(t))./std(t);
```

```
      for k=1:Hx
         reps(k,:)=polyfit(t,x(k,:),4);
      end
   end
   if opt==2   %representation DFT
     x_cf=fft(x');
     x_tcf=x_cf(1:16,:)';
     x_cf_r=real(x_tcf);
     x_cf_i=imag(x_tcf(:,2:16));
     reps=[x_cf_r x_cf_i];
   end
   if opt==3   %representaton PLS
     [Hx,Wx]=size(x);
     n=floor(Wx/10);
     Ix=floor(Wx/n);
     Mx=mod(Wx,n);
     reps=[];
     for c1=1:Ix
       reps=[reps, mean(x(:,(c1*n-n+1):(c1*n)),2),...
         std(x(:,(c1*n-n+1):(c1*n)),0,2)];
     end
     if Mx > 0
       reps=[reps, mean(x(:,(Wx-Mx+1):Wx),2), ...
         std(x(:,(Wx-Mx+1):Wx),0,2)];
     end
   end
   if opt==4   %representaton PDWT
     [Hx,Wx]=size(x);
     n=floor(Wx/10);
     Ix=floor(Wx/n);
     Mx=mod(Wx,n);
     reps=[];
     t=1:n;
     t=(t-mean(t))./std(t);
     for k=1:Hx
       buff=[];
       for c1=1:Ix
         [c,l] = wavedec(x(k,(c1*n-n+1):(c1*n)),3,'db1');
         cA3 = appcoef(c,l,'db1',3);
         cD1 = detcoef(c,l,1);
         buff=[buff,cA3,cD1];
       end
       reps(k,:)=buff;
     end
   end
%%%%%%%%%%%%%%%%%%%%%%%%%%%%%%%%%%%%%%%%%%%%%%%%%%%%%%%%%%%%%%%%%
function cls=partition_ensem(x,cnt)
x_dim = size(x,1);
```

```
for p=1:cnt
  fprintf('partitioning.%d .....\n', p);
  kn=ceil(3+randn(2)); %k*=3
  if kn<2
    kn=2;
  end
  [op,ctr,g]=kMeansCluster(x,kn);
  cn=label(g);
  cls(p,:)=cn;
end
%%%%%%%%%%%%%%%%%%%%%%%%%%%%%%%%%%%%%%%%%%%%%%%%%%%%%%%%%%%%%%%%
function cl = WCE(cls,data)
clu(1,:)=DVI_P(cls,data);
disp(['consensus partition.1......done']);
clu(2,:)=MHT_P(cls,data);
disp(['consensus partition.2......done ']);
clu(3,:)=NMI_P(cls);
disp(['consensus partition.3......done ']);
clus=[clu(1,:); clu(2,:); clu(3,:)];
cl=AGREE_F(clus,clu);
%%%%%%%%%%%%%%%%%%%%%%%%%%%%%%%%%%%%%%%%%%%%%%%%%%%%%%%%%%%%%%%%
function label = DVI_P(cls,data)
s=zeros(size(cls,2));
for i=1:size(cls,1)
  buff = cltoclb(cls(i,:));
  b_clb(:,:,i)= buff'*buff;
  index(i)=DVI(cls(i,:),data);
end;
for i=1:size(cls,1)
  w(i)=index(i)/sum(index);
  wclb(:,:,i)=b_clb(:,:,i).*w(i);
  s=s+wclb(:,:,i);
end
n=size(s,1);
x=ones(n,n);
s=x-s;
%% DSPA
Y=[];
for j=1:n-1
  Y=[Y,s(j,(j+1):n)];
end
Z= linkage(Y,'average');
[h w]=size(Z);
for i=1:h-1
  lifetime(i)=Z(i+1,w)-Z(i,w);
end
ma=find(lifetime==max(lifetime));
thres=Z(ma,w)+(Z(ma+1,w)-Z(ma,w))*rand;
clu=cluster(Z,'CUTOFF',thres,'CRITERION','distance');
label=clu';
%%%%%%%%%%%%%%%%%%%%%%%%%%%%%%%%%%%%%%%%%%%%%%%%%%%%%%%%%%%%%%%%
```

```
function label = MHT_P(cls,data)
s=zeros(size(cls,2));
for i=1:size(cls,1)
  buff = cltoclb(cls(i,:));
  b_clb(:,:,i)= buff'*buff;
  index(i)=MHT(cls(i,:),data,1);
end;
for i=1:size(cls,1)
  w(i)=index(i)/sum(index);
  wclb(:,:,i)=b_clb(:,:,i).*w(i);
  s=s+wclb(:,:,i);
end
n=size(s,1);
x=ones(n,n);
s=x-s;
%% DSPA
Y=[];
for j=1:n-1
  Y=[Y,s(j,(j+1):n)];
end
Z= linkage(Y, 'average');
[h w]=size(Z);
for i=1:h-1
  lifetime(i)=Z(i+1,w)-Z(i,w);
end
ma=find(lifetime==max(lifetime));
thres=Z(ma,w)+(Z(ma+1,w)-Z(ma,w))*rand;
clu=cluster(Z,'CUTOFF',thres,'CRITERION','distance');
label=clu';
%%%%%%%%%%%%%%%%%%%%%%%%%%%%%%%%%%%%%%%%%%%%%%%%%%%%%%%%%%%%%%%%%
function label = NMI_P(cls)
s=zeros(size(cls,2));
for i=1:size(cls,1)
  buff = cltoclb(cls(i,:));
  b_clb(:,:,i)= buff'*buff;
  index(i)=ceevalmutual(cls,cls(i,:));
end;
for i=1:size(cls,1)
  w(i)=index(i)/sum(index);
  wclb(:,:,i)=b_clb(:,:,i).*w(i);
  s=s+wclb(:,:,i);
end
n=size(s,1);
x=ones(n,n);
s=x-s;
%% DSPA
Y=[];
```

```
for j=1:n-1
  Y=[Y,s(j,(j+1):n)];
end
Z= linkage(Y, 'average');
[h w]=size(Z);
for i=1:h-1
  lifetime(i)=Z(i+1,w)-Z(i,w);
end
ma=find(lifetime==max(lifetime));
thres=Z(ma,w)+(Z(ma+1,w)-Z(ma,w))*rand;
clu=cluster(Z,'CUTOFF',thres,'CRITERION','distance');
label=clu';
%%%%%%%%%%%%%%%%%%%%%%%%%%%%%%%%%%%%%%%%%%%%%%%%%%%%%%%%%%%%%%%%
function cl = AGREE_F(cls,k)
clbs = clstoclbs(cls);
s = clbs' * clbs;
s = checks(s./size(cls,1));
n=size(s,1);
x=ones(n,n);
s=x-s;
%% DSPA
Y=[];
for j=1:n-1
  Y=[Y,s(j,(j+1):n)];
end
Z= linkage(Y,'complete');
[h w]=size(Z);
for i=1:h-1
  lifetime(i)=Z(i+1,w)-Z(i,w);
end
ma=find(lifetime==max(lifetime));
thres=Z(ma,w)+(Z(ma+1,w)-Z(ma,w))*rand;
thres=max(thres);
cl = cluster(Z,'Cutoff',thres,'Criterion','distance');
%%%%%%%%%%%%%%%%%%%%%%%%%%%%%%%%%%%%%%%%%%%%%%%%%%%%%%%%%%%%%%%%
function dun=DVI(struc,data)
class_n=max(struc);
buff=0;
for i=1:class_n
  l=find(struc==i);
  corr=corrcoef(data(:,l));
  dist=((1-corr)/2).^0.5;
  dia(i)=max(max(dist));
end
max_dia=max(dia);
for i=1:class_n-1
  for j=i+1:class_n
    li=find(struc==i);
    lj=find(struc==j);
    si=max(size(li));
    sj=max(size(lj));
```

```
      datai=data(:,li);
      dataj=data(:,lj);
      ri=[1:si];
      rj=[si+1:si+sj];
      co=corrcoef([datai dataj]);
      dis=((1-co)/2).^0.5;
      midis=min(min(dis(ri,rj)));
      buff=[buff midis];
   end
end
bs=max(size(buff));
min_dist=min(buff(2:bs));
dun=min_dist/max_dia;
%%%%%%%%%%%%%%%%%%%%%%%%%%%%%%%%%%%%%%%%%%%%%%%%%%%%%%%%%%%%%%%%%%
function mht=MHT(struc,data)
buff=0;
class_n=max(struc);
n=max(size(struc));
Q=zeros(n);
P=((1-corrcoef(data))/2).^0.5;
for i=1:class_n-1
  for j=i+1:class_n
    li=find(struc==i);
    lj=find(struc==j);
    ctri=mean(data(:,li),2);
    ctrj=mean(data(:,lj),2);
    ctr=[ctri ctrj];
    Q(li,lj)=(pdist(ctr','correlation')/2).^0.5;
    Q(lj,li)=(pdist(ctr','correlation')/2).^0.5;
  end
end
mht=sum(sum((P.*Q)))/(n*(n-1));
%%%%%%%%%%%%%%%%%%%%%%%%%%%%%%%%%%%%%%%%%%%%%%%%%%%%%%%%%%%%%%%%%%
function nmi = ceevalmutual(cls,cl),
nmi = 0;
totinds = 0;
n = length(cl);
for i=1:size(cls,1),
  inds = find(isfinite(cls(i,:)));
  q(i) = evalmutual(checkcl(cl(inds)),checkcl(cls(i,inds)));
  nmi = q(i)*length(inds) + nmi;
  totinds = totinds + length(inds);
end;
nmi = nmi/totinds;
%%%%%%%%%%%%%%%%%%%%%%%%%%%%%%%%%%%%%%%%%%%%%%%%%%%%%%%%%%%%%%%%%%
% The other functions(ClusterEnsemble Toolbox) are downloaded
% http://www.lans.ece.utexas.edu/~strehl/soft.html
```

References

Ailon N, Charikar M, et al. Aggregating inconsistent information: ranking and clustering. Journal of the ACM (JACM) 2008;55(5):1–27.

Akaike H. A new look at the statistical model identification. IEEE Transactions on Automatic Control 1974;19(6):716–23.

Al-Razgan M, Domeniconi C. Weighted clustering ensembles. In: Proceedings of SIAM international conference on data mining; 2006.

Analoui M, Sadighian N. Solving cluster ensemble problems by correlation's matrix & GA. Intelligent Information Processing 2007;III:227–31.

Ankerst M, Breunig M, et al. OPTICS: ordering points to identify the clustering structure. In: ACM-SIGMOD international conference on management of data; 1999.

Attili JB, Savic M, et al. A TMS32020-based real time, text-independent, automatic speaker verification system. In: Proceedings of international conference on acoustics, speech, signal processing; 1988.

Azimi J, Abdoos M, et al. A new efficient approach in clustering ensembles. IDEAL LNCS. 2007.

Azimi J, Mohammadi M, et al. Clustering ensembles using genetic algorithm. In: IEEE the international workshop on computer architecture for machine perception and sensing; 2006.

Bagnall A, Janacek G. Clustering time series from ARMA models with clipped data. In: Proceedings of the international conference on knowledge discovery in data and data mining, Seattle, USA; 2004.

Bagnall A, Janacek G. Clustering time series with clipped data. Machine Learning 2005; 58(2):151–78.

Bagnall A, Ratanamahatana CA, et al. A bit level representation for time series data mining with shape based similarity. Data Mining and Knowledge Discovery 2006;13(1):11–40.

Banfield JD, Raftery AE. Model-based Gaussian and non-Gaussian clustering. Biometrics 1993;49(3):803–21.

Bar-Hillel A, Hertz T, et al. Learning a mahalanobis metric from equivalence constraints. Journal of Machine Learning Research 2006;6(1):937.

Bashir F. MotionSearch: object motion trajectory-based video database system-index, retrieval, classification and recognition [Ph.D. thesis]. Chicago (USA): Dept. Elect. Eng., Univ. of Illinois; 2005.

Baum LE, Eagon J. An inequality with applications to statistical estimation for probabilistic functions of Markov processes and to a model for ecology. Bulletin of the American Mathematical Society 1967;73(3):360–3.

Baum LE, Sell GR. Growth transformations for functions on manifolds. Pacific Journal of Mathematics 1968;27(2):211–27.

Beran J, Mazzola G. Visualizing the relationship between time series by hierarchical smoothing models. Journal of Computational and Graphical Statistics 1999;8(2):213–38.

Bezdek JC. Pattern recognition with fuzzy objective function algorithms. Kluwer Academic Publishers; 1981.

Bilmes JA. A gentle tutorial of the EM algorithm and its application to parameter estimation for Gaussian mixture and hidden Markov models. International Computer Science Institute; 1998. 4.

Breiman L. Bagging predictors. Machine Learning 1996a;24(2):123–40.

Breiman L. Stacked regressions. Machine Learning 1996b;24(1):49–64.

Brown G. Ensemble learning, encyclopedia of machine learning. 2009.

Brown G, Yao X, et al. Exploiting ensemble diversity for automatic feature extraction. 2002.

Butler M. Hidden Markov model clustering of acoustic data [M.Sc. thesis]. School of Informatics, University of Edinburgh; 2003.

CAVIAR. Context aware vision using image-based active recognition [online]. 2002. Available: http://homepages.inf.ed.ac.uk/rbf/CAVIAR.

Chakrabarti K, Keogh E, et al. Locally adaptive dimensionality reduction for indexing large time series databases. ACM Transactions on Database Systems (TODS) 2002;27(2):228.

Chang H. A survey of model-based clustering algorithms for sequential data [Ph.D. thesis]. Hong Kong University of Science and Technology; 2002.

Chen K. A connectionist method for pattern classification with diverse features. Pattern Recognition Letters 1998;19(7):545−58.

Chen K. On the dynamic pattern analysis, discovery and recognition [online]. 2005. Available: http://www.ieeesmc.org/Newsletter/sep2005/CHEN.php.

Chen K. On the use of different speech representations for speaker modeling. IEEE Transactions on Systems, Man, and Cybernetics Part C: Applications and Reviews 2005b;35(3):301.

Chen K, Chi H. A method of combining multiple probabilistic classifiers through soft competition on different feature sets. Neurocomputing 1998;20(1−3):227−52.

Chen K, Wang L, et al. Methods of combining multiple classifiers with different features and their applications to text-independent speaker identification. International Journal of Pattern Recognition and Artificial Intelligence 1997;11(3):417−46.

Chen W, Chang SF. Motion trajectory matching of video objects. Proceedings of IS&T/SPIE Conference on Storage and Retrieval for Media Databases 2000.

Cheng H, Hua KA, et al. Constrained locally weighted clustering. Proceedings of the VLDB Endowment 2008;1(1):90−101.

Cheong CW, Wei Lee W, et al. Wavelet-based temporal cluster analysis on stock time series. ICOQSIA 2005;2005:6−8.

Cho SB, Kim JH. Multiple network fusion using fuzzy logic. IEEE Transactions on Neural Networks 1995;6(2):497−501.

Colombi J, Ruck D, et al. Cohort selection and word grammar effects for speaker recognition. In: Proceedings of international conference on acoustics, speech, signal processing; 1996.

Cox MG, Ei C, et al. The generalized weighted mean of correlated quantities. Metrologia 2006;43:S268.

Cunningham P, Carney J. Diversity versus quality in classification ensembles based on feature selection. Machine Learning: ECML 2000;2000:109−16.

Davies DL, Bouldin DW. A cluster separation measure. IEEE Transactions on Pattern Analysis and Machine Intelligence 1979;1(2):95−104.

Dempster AP, Laird NM, et al. Maximum likelihood from incomplete data via the EM algorithm. Journal of the Royal Statistical Society. Series B (Methodological) 1977;39(1):1−38.

Denton A. Kernel-density-based clustering of time series subsequences using a continuous random-walk noise model. In: Proceedings of IEEE international conference on data mining, Houston, USA; 2005.

Dimitrova N, Golshani F. Motion recovery for video content classification. ACM Transactions on Information Systems (TOIS) 1995;13(4):408−39.

Ding H, Trajcevski G, et al. Querying and mining of time series data: experimental comparison of representations and distance measures. Proceedings of the VLDB Endowment 2008;1(2):1542−52.

Dudoit S, Fridlyand J. Bagging to improve the accuracy of a clustering procedure. Bioinformatics 2003;19(9):1090.

Dunn JC. Well-separated clusters and optimal fuzzy partitions. Cybernetics and Systems 1974;4(1):95–104.

Ester M, Kriegel HP, et al. A density-based algorithm for discovering clusters in large spatial databases with noise. In: Proceedings of international conference on knowledge discovery and data mining; 1996.

Faloutsos C, Ranganathan M, et al. Fast subsequence matching in time-series databases. In: Proceedings of ACM SIGMOD conference; 1994.

Fern XZ, Brodley CE. Solving cluster ensemble problems by bipartite graph partitioning. In: Proceedings of international conference on machine learning; 2004.

Fischer B, Buhmann J. Bagging for path-based clustering. In: IEEE transactions on pattern analysis and machine intelligence; 2003. p. 1411–5.

Fleiss JL. Statistical methods for rates and proportions. John Wiley & Sons; 1973.

Forgy E. Cluster analysis of multivariate data: efficiency vs. interpretability of classifications. Biometrics 1965;21(3):768.

Forney Jr GD. The viterbi algorithm. Proceedings of the IEEE 1973;61(3):268–78.

Fraley C. Algorithms for model-based Gaussian hierarchical clustering. SIAM Journal on Scientific Computing 1999;20(1):270–81.

Fraley C, Raftery AE. Model-based clustering, discriminant analysis, and density estimation. Journal of the American Statistical Association 2002;97(458):611–31.

Fred A. Finding consistent clusters in data partitions. Multiple Classifier Systems 2001: 309–18.

Fred ALN, Jain AK. Combining multiple clusterings using evidence accumulation. In: IEEE transactions on pattern analysis and machine intelligence; 2005. p. 835–50.

Freund Y, Schapire RE. A decision-theoretic generalization of on-line learning and an application to boosting. Journal of Computer and System Sciences 1997;55(1):119–39.

Frossyniotis D, Likas A, et al. A clustering method based on boosting. Pattern Recognition Letters 2004;25(6):641–54.

Gavrilov M, Anguelov D, et al. Mining the stock market: which measure is best. In: Proceedings of international conference on knowledge discovery and data mining; 2000.

Ghaemi R, Sulaiman MN, et al. A survey: clustering ensembles techniques. World Academy of Science, Engineering and Technology; 2009.

Giacinto G, Roli F. Design of effective neural network ensembles for image classification purposes. Image and Vision Computing 2001;19(9–10):699–707.

Gionis A, Mannila H, et al. Clustering aggregation. ACM Transactions on Knowledge Discovery from Data (TKDD) 2007;1(1):4.

Grunwald P, Kontkanen P, et al. Minimum encoding approaches for predictive modeling. In: Proceedings of the fourteenth international conference on uncertainty in AI; 1998.

Guha S, Rastogi R, et al. CURE: an efficient clustering algorithm for large databases. In: Proceedings of ACM SIGMOD international conference on management of data; 1998.

Halkidi M, Batistakis Y, et al. On clustering validation techniques. Journal of Intelligent Information Systems 2001;17(2):107–45.

Halkidi M, Batistakis Y, et al. Cluster validity methods: part I. ACM SIGMOD Record 2002; 31(2):40–5.

Halkidi M, Vazirgiannis M. Clustering validity assessment: finding the optimal partitioning of a data set. In: Proceedings of the IEEE international conference on data mining; 2001.

Hansen LK, Salamon P. Neural network ensembles. In: IEEE transactions on pattern analysis and machine intelligence, vol. 12(10); 1990. p. 993–1001.

Ho TK. The random subspace method for constructing decision forests. In: IEEE transactions on pattern analysis and machine intelligence, vol. 20(8); 1998. p. 832–44.

Ho TK, Hull JJ, et al. Decision combination in multiple classifier systems. In: IEEE transactions on pattern analysis and machine intelligence, vol. 16(1); 1994. p. 66–75.

Hoeppner F. Fuzzy cluster analysis: methods for classification, data analysis, and image recognition. Wiley; 1999.

Hong Y, Kwong S, et al. Unsupervised feature selection using clustering ensembles and population based incremental learning algorithm. Pattern Recognition 2008;41(9):2742–56.

Hu X, Xu L. A comparative study of several cluster number selection criteria. In: Proceedings of the 4th international conference on intelligent data engineering and automated learning; 2003. p. 195–202.

Huang Z. Extensions to the k-means algorithm for clustering large data sets with categorical values. Data Mining and Knowledge Discovery 1998;2(3):283–304.

Jain AK, Duin RPW, et al. Statistical pattern recognition: a review. In: IEEE transactions on pattern analysis and machine intelligence, vol. 22(1); 2000. p. 4–37.

Jain AK, Murty MN, et al. Data clustering: a review. ACM Computing Surveys (CSUR) 1999; 31(3):264–323.

Jiang D, Pei J, et al. DHC: a density-based hierarchical clustering method for time series gene expression data. In: Proceedings of the 3rd IEEE symposium on bioinformatics and bioengineering; 2003.

Johnson SC. Hierarchical clustering schemes. Psychometrika 1967;32(3):241–54.

Juang BH, Rabiner LR. A probabilistic distance measure for hidden Markov models. AT&T Bell Laboratories Technical Journal 1985;64(2):391–408.

Karypis G, Aggarwal R, et al. Multilevel hypergraph partitioning: application in VLSI domain. ACM; 1997.

Karypis G, Kumar V. A fast and high quality multilevel scheme for partitioning irregular graphs. SIAM Journal on Scientific Computing 1999;20(1):359.

Kaufman L, Rousseeuw PJ, editors. Finding groups in data: an introduction to cluster analysis. New York: Wiley; 1990.

Kellam P, Liu X, et al. Comparing, contrasting and combining clusters in viral gene expression data. In: Proceedings of 6th workshop on intelligent data analysis; 2001.

Keogh E. Temporal data mining benchmarks. 2003. http://www.cs.ucr.edu/~eamonn/time_series_data.

Keogh E, Chakrabarti K, et al. Dimensionality reduction for fast similarity search in large time series databases. Knowledge and Information Systems 2001;3(3):263–86.

Keogh E, Kasetty S. On the need for time series data mining benchmarks: a survey and empirical demonstration. Data Mining and Knowledge Discovery 2003;7(4):349–71.

Khalid S, Naftel A. Classifying spatiotemporal object trajectories using unsupervised learning of basis function coefficients. In: Proceedings of the third ACM international workshop on video surveillance & sensor networks; 2005. p. 45–52.

Kittler J, Hatef M, et al. On combining classifiers. IEEE Transactions on Pattern Analysis and Machine Intelligence 1998;20(3):226–39.

Kleinberg J. An impossibility theorem for clustering. The MIT Press; 2003.

Kohavi R, Wolpert DH. Bias plus variance decomposition for zero-one loss functions. In: Proceedings of 13th international conference on machine learning, Morgan Kaufmann; 1996.

Kotsiantis SB, Pintelas PE. Combining bagging and boosting. International Journal of Computational Intelligence 2004;1(4):324−33.

Krishnapuram R, Joshi A, et al. Low-complexity fuzzy relational clustering algorithms for web mining. IEEE Transactions on Fuzzy Systems 2001;9(4):595−607.

Kuncheva LI, Hadjitodorov ST. Using diversity in cluster ensembles. In: Proceedings of IEEE international conference on systems, man and cybernetics; 2004.

Kuncheva LI, Whitaker CJ. Measures of diversity in classifier ensembles and their relationship with the ensemble accuracy. Machine Learning 2003;51(2):181−207.

Li KP, Wrench EH. Text-independent speaker identification with short utterances. In: Proceedings of international conference on acoustics, speech, signal processing; 1983.

Li T, Ding C. Weighted consensus clustering. In: Proceedings of SIAM international conference on data mining; 2008.

Liao T, Bolt B, et al. In: Understanding and projecting the battle state. 23rd Army Science Conference, Orlando, FL; 2002.

Lin J, Keogh E, et al. Finding motifs in time series. In: Proceedings of workshop on temporal data mining; 2002.

Lin J, Vlachos M, et al. Iterative incremental clustering of time series. Advances in Database Technology - EDBT 2004;2004:521−2.

Lin W, Orgun MA, et al. An overview of temporal data mining. The Australasian Data Mining Workshop; 2002.

Liu H, Brown DE. A new point process transition density model for space-time event prediction. IEEE Transactions on Systems, Man and Cybernetics (Part C) 2004;34:310−24.

Liu Y, Jin R, et al. Boostcluster: boosting clustering by pairwise constraints. In: Proceedings of the 13th ACM SIGKDD international conference on knowledge discovery and data mining; 2007.

Luo H, Jing F, et al. Combining multiple clusterings using information theory based genetic algorithm. In: IEEE international conference on computational intelligence and security; 2006.

Monti S, Tamayo P, et al. Consensus clustering: a resampling-based method for class discovery and visualization of gene expression microarray data. Machine Learning 2003;52(1):91−118.

Murphy KP. Dynamic Bayesian networks: representation, inference and learning [Ph.D. thesis]. Berkeley: University of California; 2002. Computer Science.

Ng A, Jordan M, et al. On spectral clustering: analysis and an algorithm. Advances in Neural Information Processing Systems 2001.

Nilsson NJ. Learning machines: foundations of trainable pattern-classifying systems. New York: McGraw-Hill; 1965.

Oates T, Firoiu L, et al. Clustering time series with hidden Markov models and dynamic time warping. In: Proceedings of the IJCAI-99 workshop on neural, symbolic and reinforcement learning methods for sequence learning; 1999.

Openshaw J, Sun Z, et al. A comparison of composite features under degraded speech in speaker recognition. In: Proceedings of international conference on acoustics, speech, signal processing; 1993.

Ordonez C, Omiecinski E. Efficient disk-based K-means clustering for relational databases. IEEE Transactions on Knowledge and Data Engineering 2004;16(8):909−21.

Oza N, Tumer K. Input decimation ensembles: decorrelation through dimensionality reduction. Multiple Classifier Systems 2001:238−47.

Panuccio A, Bicego M, et al. A hidden Markov model-based approach to sequential data clustering. In: Structural, Syntactic, and statistical pattern recognition; 2009. p. 734—43.

Partridge D, Krzanowski W. Software diversity: practical statistics for its measurement and exploitation. Information and Software Technology 1997;39(10):707—17.

Pavlovic V. Model-based motion clustering using boosted mixture modeling. In: Proceedings of IEEE conference on computer vision and pattern recognition; 2004.

PDMC. In: Physiological data modeling contest workshop, international conference on machine learning 2004; 2004. http://www.cs.utexas.edu/users/sherstov/pdmc/.

Picone J. Continuous speech recognition using hidden Markov models. IEEE ASSP Magazine 1990;7(3):26—41.

Policker S, Geva AB. Nonstationary time series analysis by temporal clustering. IEEE Transactions on Systems, Man, and Cybernetics (Part B) 2000;30(2):339—43.

Raftery AE, Madigan D, et al. Bayesian model averaging for linear regression models. Journal of the American Statistical Association 1997;92(437):179—91.

Ramoni M, Sebastiani P, et al. Bayesian clustering by dynamics. Machine Learning 2002; 47(1):91—121.

Rodrigues PP, Gama J, et al. Hierarchical clustering of time-series data streams. IEEE Transactions on Knowledge and Data Engineering 2008;20(5):615—27.

Saffari A, Bischof H. Clustering in a boosting framework. In: Proceedings of computer vision winter workshop; 2007.

Sahouria E, Zakhor A. Motion indexing of video. In: Proceedings of IEEE international conference on image processing; 1997.

Schapire RE. A brief introduction to boosting. In: Proceedings of the sixteenth international joint conference on artificial intelligence. Morgan Kaufmann; 1999.

Schwarz G. Estimating the dimension of a model. The Annals of Statistics 1978;6(2):461—4.

Sharkey AJC. Combining artificial neural nets: ensemble and modular multi-net systems. Multi-Net Systems, Springer-Verlag; 1999. p. 1—30.

Sharma S. Applied multivariate techniques. New York, NY, USA: John Wiley & Sons, Inc.; 1995.

Singh V, Mukherjee L, et al. Ensemble clustering using semidefinite programming. Advances in Neural Information Processing Systems 2007.

Sinkkonen J, Kaski S. Clustering based on conditional distributions in an auxiliary space. Neural Computation 2002;14(1):217—39.

Skalak DB. The sources of increased accuracy for two proposed boosting algorithms. In: Proceedings of American association for artificial intelligence, AAAI-96, integrating multiple learned models workshop; 1996.

Smyth P. Clustering using Monte Carlo cross-validation. In: Proceedings of the second international conference on knowledge discovery and data mining; 1996.

Smyth P. Clustering sequences with hidden Markov models. In: Advances in neural information processing systems; 1997. p. 648—54.

Smyth P. Probabilistic model-based clustering of multivariate and sequential data. In: Proceedings of the seventh international workshop on artificial intelligence and statistics; 1999.

Souvenir R, Pless R. Manifold clustering. In: Proceedings of IEEE international conference on computer vision; 2005.

Strehl A, Ghosh J. Cluster ensembles—a knowledge reuse framework for combining multiple partitions. The Journal of Machine Learning Research 2003;3:583—617.

Sun R, Giles CL. Sequence learning: paradigms, algorithms, and applications. In: Number 1828 in Lecture Notes in Artificial Intelligence. Springer-Verlag; 2000.

Theodoridis S, Koutroumbas K, et al. Pattern recognition. Academic Press; 1999.

Tibshirani R, Knight K. The covariance inflation criterion for adaptive model selection. Journal of the Royal Statistical Society: Series B (Statistical Methodology) 1999;61(3): 529–46.

Topchy A, Jain AK, et al. Combining multiple weak clusterings. In: Proceedings of the third IEEE international conference on data mining; 2003.

Topchy A, Minaei-Bidgoli B, et al. Adaptive clustering ensembles. Pattern Recognition 2004; 1:272–5.

Topchy AP, Law MHC, et al. Analysis of consensus partition in cluster ensemble. In: Proceedings of IEEE international conference on data mining; 2004.

Tumer K, Oza NC. Input decimated ensembles. Pattern Analysis & Applications 2003;6(1): 65–77.

Van Wijk J, Van Selow E. Cluster and calendar based visualization of time series data. In: Proceedings of IEEE symposium on information visualization, San Francisco, CA; 1999.

Vinh N, Epps J, et al. Information theoretic measures for clusterings comparison: is a correction for chance necessary?. In: Proceedings of the 26th international conference on machine learning (ICML'09); 2009.

Viswanath P, Jayasurya K. A fast and efficient ensemble clustering method. Pattern Recognition 2006;2:720–3.

Viterbi A. Error bounds for convolutional codes and an asymptotically optimum decoding algorithm. IEEE Transactions on Information Theory 1967;13(2):260–9.

Vlachos M, Lin J, et al. A wavelet-based anytime algorithm for k-means clustering of time series. In: Proceedings of the third SIAM international conference on data mining, San Francisco, CA; 2003.

Wang S, Chen K. Ensemble learning with active data selection for semi-supervised pattern classification. In: Proceedings of international joint conference on neural networks; 2007.

Ward Jr JH. Hierarchical grouping to optimize an objective function. Journal of the American Statistical Association 1963;58(301):236–44.

Weingessel A, Dimitriadou E, et al. An ensemble method for clustering. Working paper. 2003.

Winston WL, Goldberg JB. Operations research: applications and algorithms. 1994.

Wittner BS, Denker JS. Strategies for teaching layered networks classification tasks. In: Anderson DZ, editor. Neural information processing systems, USA; 1988.

Xiong Y, Yeung DY. Mixtures of ARMA models for model-based time series clustering. In: Proceedings of IEEE international conference on data mining; 2002.

Xu L. A unified learning scheme: Bayesian-Kullback Ying-Yang machines. In: Proceedings of advances in neural information processing systems; 1996.

Xu L. Bayesian Ying-Yang machine, clustering and number of clusters. Pattern Recognition Letters 1997;18(11–13):1167–78.

Xu R, Wunsch D. Survey of clustering algorithms. IEEE Transactions on Neural Networks 2005;16(3):645–78.

Yang Y. Clustering ensemble with multiple representations for temporal data clustering [M.Phil]. School of Informatics, University of Manchester; 2006.

Yang Y, Chen K. An ensemble of competitive learning learning networks with different representations for temporal data clustering. In: Proceedings of international joint conference on neural networks Vancouver, Canada; 2006.

Yang Y, Chen K. Combining competitive learning networks on various representations for temporal data clustering. In: Trends in neural computation. Springer; 2007. p. 315–36.

Yang Y, Chen K. Unsupervised learning via iteratively constructed clustering ensemble. In: Proceedings of international joint conference on neural networks, Barcelona, Spain; 2010.

Yang Y, Chen K. Temporal data clustering via weighted clustering ensemble with different representations. IEEE Transactions on Knowledge and Data Engineering 2011a;23(2): 307–20.

Yang Y, Chen K. Time series clustering via RPCL network ensemble with different representations. IEEE Transactions on Systems, Man, and Cybernetics, Part C: Applications and Reviews 2011b;99:1–10.

Ye L, Keogh E. Time series shapelets: a new primitive for data mining. SIGKDD. 2009.

Zhang T, Ramakrishnan R, et al. BIRCH: an efficient data clustering method for very large databases. In: Proceedings of ACM SIGMOD international conference on management of data; 1996.

Zhong S, Ghosh J. A unified framework for model-based clustering. The Journal of Machine Learning Research 2003;4:1037.

Zucchini W. An introduction to model selection. Journal of Mathematical Psychology 2000; 44(1):41–61.

Index

Printed in the United States
By Bookmasters